Up On Preston Mountain

Up On Preston Mountain

The Story of an American Ghost Town

John F. Polhemus

Richard V. Polhemus

PURPLE MOUNTAIN PRESS
Fleischmanns, New York

To the memory of Gayle Polhemus
For Maria Polhemus
To the Memory of John and Gertrude Polhemus

Up On Preston Mountain: The Story of an American Ghost Town

First Edition 2005

Published by
Purple Mountain Press, Ltd.
P.O. Box 309, Fleischmanns, New York 12430-0309
845-254-4062, 845-254-4476 (fax)
purple@catskill.net   www.catskill.net/purple

ISBN 1-930098-68-5

Library of Congress Control Number 2005908773

Cover lithograph, *At Home in the Wilderness*,
by Currier & Ives, 1870

Cover design by Janet Atkins, Hinterland Design, Coxsackie, NY

Photographs and maps by Julie Polhemus

Manufactured in the United States of America on acid-free paper
5 4 3 2 1

Contents

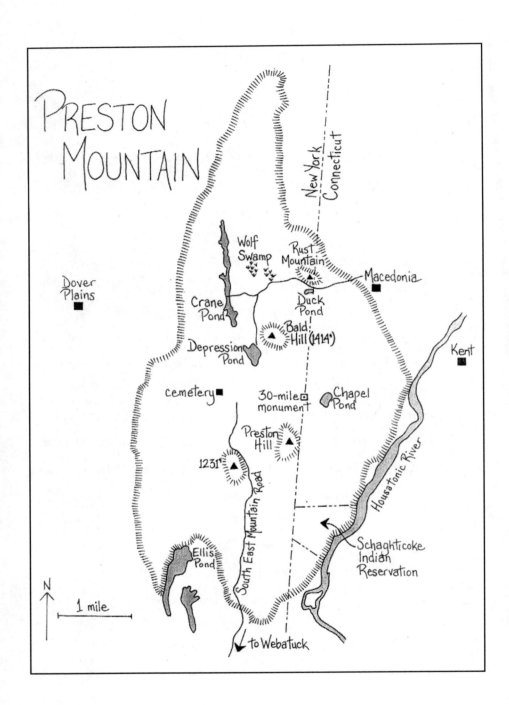

PRESTON MOUNTAIN

New York
Connecticut

Wolf Swamp

Rust Mountain

Macedonia

Dover Plains

Crane Pond

Duck Pond

Bald Hill (1414')

Depression Pond

Kent

cemetery

30-mile monument

Chapel Pond

Preston Hill

Housatonic River

1231'

South East Mountain Road

Ellis Pond

Schaghticoke Indian Reservation

N

1 mile

to Webatuck

Preface

THE *POUGHKEEPSIE SUNDAY COURIER* of November 12, 1922, featured an article entitled "First and Last on Preston Mountain— Some Interesting Records of a Once Populous Community in the Town of Dover, Now Little More Than a Memory—Glimpse of the Past." A photograph accompanied the article: two elderly men and a girl standing in front of an old house with a massive stone chimney. They were Erben Kennedy, Milton Preston, and Milton's daughter Evangeline. Erben and Milton were distant cousins, both great-great-grandsons of Martin and Rebecca Preston, the first permanent settlers on Preston Mountain.

Milton and Evangeline lived elsewhere—off the Mountain. They were visiting the homesites of their ancestors. Erben Kennedy, a bachelor, lived in the old house on Preston Mountain. The photo shows Erben as a lean, hatchet-faced old man, standing erect with a cane, and staring fixedly into the camera. The article's author, Arthur T. Benson, described Erben as, "a genial, benevolent old gentleman, somewhat modest and retiring, because, perhaps, of the secluded life he has led. Our party was hospitably received by him on the hot September afternoon of our pilgrimage and treated to a home brew of old fashioned root beer." Erben was a friendly hermit, living atop Preston Mountain alone.

Erben was noted for walking his horse down the mountain every month or so (if the weather permitted) to replenish his supplies and to check the mail. One visitor noted that when a rattlesnake rested on his front doorstep, he walked around it so as not to disturb it. His brothers and sisters, all teachers in Connecticut, visited him occasionally, and their children remembered him and his way of life fondly. If he was a little odd, they loved him for it. When he died in 1924, the last of the old Preston Mountain community disappeared.

After Erben died, stories and myths grew up about the mountain. Miles of stone walls, old roads, cellar holes, and a brush-clogged cemetery were all that remained of the old community. It was thought that those people must have been peculiar to live way out there in the woods. But it was a place and a way of life that appealed to us, two boys from the valley.

Our parents introduced us to the mountain fifty years ago, rambling with us through the cemetery and past old foundations. We cooked steaks over a wood fire. We searched for a lost collie on a snowy Christmas Eve (he turned up, hungry but healthy, on the back porch two days later). We took up exploring by ourselves as teenagers, got lost in a fog, hung up a Ford on a rock on the mountain road, and felt the chill of a zero-degree day as the wind whistled through the oaks on a ridge top. One of us hunted deer in the swamps and hemlock woods beyond the stone walls. The lure of the mountain remained in us long after these experiences. But we knew nothing of the people who built the walls, lived in the houses over the cellar holes, or were buried in the cemetery. We promised ourselves that someday we would find out about them.

When we began research for this book it seemed an impossible task. It was clear that, at least in the early years, most of the Mountain people had been illiterate. The few recorded deeds were usually marked with an "x" for a signature; most land transfers were never recorded. The Mountain people left no diaries, no letters, and no memorials from admirers to help historians. It seemed that the story of Preston Mountain was left blank.

As we conducted our research, sources appeared that we had not imagined. The early history was available in documents in the New York State Archives and the New-York Historical Society. Much was recorded in deeds in Kent, Connecticut, and in the proceedings of the General Assembly of Connecticut. We found family genealogies, military pension records, and census records. Descendants of Mountain residents appeared on the Internet. The story began to reveal itself. The history of the people on all sides of the Mountain was well documented. It became clear that the Mountain people were the poor and dispossessed, and neighbors who were relatively affluent surrounded them. Thus, the Mountain's history became a story of conflict—not always of conflict between people (though it was that sometimes), but of conflict between ways of life. The mercantile and industrial interests of the surrounding valleys intruded on the subsistence farms of the Mountain, and the result, predictably, was disaster for the farmers.

There was more to the story; it was written in the character of the people. The conflict and hardship of life on the Mountain fostered a brave and resourceful people. Their stories deserved to be told. Frederick Jackson Turner wrote that history was often, "the brilliant annals of the few"—accounts of courts and knights and palaces. "But history has its tragedy as well, which tells of the degraded tillers of the soil, toiling that others might dream, the slavery that rendered possible the 'glory that was Greece'—these as well demand their annals."[2]

In the service of full disclosure, it should be noted that the authors are descended from two of the men who figure in the story of Preston Mountain—Ebenezer Preston Jr. and Nathan Soule. It is human nature to suppose that one's ancestors lived upright and honorable lives, and we are not exceptions to that instinct. There appeared to be no blemish on Soule's record. But readers may have to make some hard decisions about the actions of Ebenezer Preston Jr. To this we can only refer to the aphorism about turning over rocks.

Chapter One
Preston Mountain Today

PRESTON MOUNTAIN IS A MASSIF—A HIGH UPLAND. It rises between the Housatonic River valley in Kent, Connecticut, and the TenMile River valley in Dover, New York, split nearly in half by the state border. The northern tip of the Mountain lies in Amenia, New York. It is roughly eight miles in length, from north to south, and three and a half miles in width at its widest point. Thick in the middle, the Mountain narrows at both ends, like an upside down lifeboat.

The name, "Preston Mountain," is a name of convenience. People in New York call it "East Mountain," and so it is named on the Geological Survey map. In Kent, it was called "West Mountain" or "Dover Mountain." The Indians called it "Schaghticoke Mountain." Each of these names has a legitimate claim for primacy. Another old name that is never used today, and, in fact, is almost entirely unknown is "the Hoveout." So, using the name "Preston Mountain" is a compromise to avoid confusion, but there are reasons for the name. The Preston family arrived early and stayed the longest; the highest point is "Preston Hill," 1,450 feet on the topographical map; the largest landowner in both states is the Preston Mountain Club.

From the valleys on either side, the Mountain rises seven or eight hundred feet in a steep escarpment around its entire perimeter. The only public road runs north and south in a narrow valley from Dogtail Corners to a dead end near an old farmhouse. This road is also the only gradual approach to the Mountain. All other roads (none of which are open to the public) climb steeply from the valleys. Some follow streambeds through ravines between the hills. Others zigzag up the face of the escarpment. All of these roads were laid out for travel by foot, horses, or oxen. Some are still passable by jeep or all-terrain vehicle. Most are closed and gated.

The Mountain is, in a sense, a plateau—an elevated tract of more or less level land. However, the upland is pierced by even higher hills rising four or five hundred feet above the surrounding countryside. The tops of these hills are less thickly forested than the lower land, clad with stunted and wind-twisted oaks and conifers. From the highest of these hills, on a clear day, one can see the Catskills. Mountain laurel overruns the steep, boulder-strewn hillsides, forming impenetrable thickets, and providing cover for deer, bear, wildcats, and coyotes.

Ponds and swamps dot the landscape. All of the ponds are manmade. Crane Pond, the largest, is a long, riverlike lake in Dover and Amenia. The Crane family dammed it at the north end early in the twentieth century. The east side of the lake is bounded by unbroken forest from one end of the pond to the other. There is one log cabin on the west shore. A road crosses Crane Pond on a bridge and causeway at the site of a much older bridge known as "Kennedy Bridge" (which was often misspelled as "Canaday Bridge"). Before the stream was dammed, its name was "Kennedy Bridge Brook." Today it is called "Roaring Brook" for its noisy descent into the valley to the west.

Depression Pond lies in a bowl beneath high peaks, southeast of Crane Pond. Chapel Pond rests in a similar valley just over the border in Kent. Parts of old farms lie submerged beneath all three ponds.

Considerable streams spring from the ponds and swamps. Roaring Brook springs from Crane Pond. Bolt Brook (also called Preston Mountain Brook) rises at Depression Pond and flows first north, then east, through Duck Pond, and down the steep, rocky ravine to Macedonia. Thayer Brook issues from Chapel Pond and rushes to the Housatonic, south of Mount Algo. Several streams rise in swamps, including "Mortmeadow Brook," which runs west within a rod of the doorstep of the Mountain's first settler.

Wolf Swamp, east of Crane Pond, is unnamed on the topographical map. Old deeds confirm that it has been called "Wolf Swamp" for almost two centuries, and, likely, much longer than that. Tamarack Swamp occupies a deep hollow in the hills near the south end of the Mountain. In recent years, beaver have made a strong comeback. Their dams enlarge the swamps, spilling them over roads and trails and flooding the surrounding woods. Many former bogs are now ponds, spiked with the whitening trunks of dead trees.[1]

The Mountain is heavily forested from the valley floors almost to the crests of the highest hills. Most of the forest is oak and beech, sprinkled with clumps of birch. Sugar maples line old roads and fields. White pines soar over the ridge tops. North of Wolf Swamp is an extensive hemlock forest. Some of these hemlocks are very large, and the ground beneath them is shaded and silent.

It is tempting to think that some isolated pockets of this forest might be first growth timber were it not for the presence everywhere of leveled rings of earth. These rings mark where stacks of wood were burned into charcoal in the iron-making days. Those who made them called them "coal bottoms" or "coal pits"—leveled circles of earth twenty to thirty feet in diameter. No part of Preston Mountain is without them.

These coal bottoms cover all the mountains in the old iron region of northwest Connecticut and eastern New York. Near Bull's Bridge, the Appalachian Trail climbs the southeast flank of Preston Mountain behind the Schaghticoke Indian Reservation. The distance to the top of the mountain from Schaghticoke Road is about a mile. In that mile, the trail crosses six coal bottoms and is within sight of ten more. The abundance of these places suggests that there was a time when the forests were clear-cut and the land was bare on Preston Mountain and elsewhere in the iron region.

Of necessity, a road passed near each coal pit. Colliers, woodsmen, and teamsters loaded the charcoal into four-wheeled, oxen-drawn, charcoal wagons to be hauled to the forge or furnace. Today it is difficult to distinguish these roads in the forest; but they are there. The best charcoal roads angled up the mountains at a moderate pitch. Boulder fields, swamps, and cliffs often compelled the roads to be built straight up and down the slopes. Many of these roads became watercourses during heavy runoff. Freshets and meltwater scoured the soil, leaving sunken, rock-strewn channels.

Erosion became a problem on the Mountain, perhaps even a catastrophic problem. There are deep, V-shaped ditches, slicing down the steeper hillsides. Such ditches are common throughout the iron region.

They were probably seasonal streambeds, dry most of the year. At some point, extraordinary volumes of water raced down them, carving out great scars in the mountainside. They rarely run water today.

Stone walls penetrate the woods on the Mountain. Constructed by years of labor from men, boys, and oxen, the walls outline old meadows, pasture, and tillage. The pioneers called them "fences," not "walls," emphasizing their use in an agricultural society. Ancient plow land still reveals the back furrows—sunken trenches running down the center of a field or a wave of plowed ground resting against a wall. Deep in the hemlock forest, a stone fence blocks one end of a steep, wild ravine. Walls seem to end for no apparent reason; the connecting wooden bars or brush fence have long since rotted away.

Swamps and rough, rocky hillsides separate one system of walls from another—one abandoned farm from another. Usually, a cellar hole remains near the center of each pattern of walls. These are shallow, leaf-filled depressions, sometimes containing the tumbled remains of the stone chimney and foundation. The cellar was usually smaller than the house above it. Sometimes, the outline of the old house can be seen in the patterns of foundation stones, doorsteps, and cellar stairs. Of the poorer cabins, with earth floors and stick-and-mud chimneys, nothing remains. Around the homesites, walls outline the locations of the dooryard and the nearby barnyard. None of these homes were far from some kind of road, no matter how rough. It requires imagination to find the roads today.

Sugar maple trees appear near the abandoned farms. They line the roads and fields. There is a living maple tree, fully six feet in diameter, across the road from the ruins of Martin Preston's house. There are few maples in the outlying, predominant oak forest. On Preston Mountain, the maple is a marker of human presence, perhaps descended from trees the settlers planted to make sugar.

Apple trees also appear near the ruins. These trees are the descendants of those planted generations ago. Some of them bear sizeable yields of fruit—big green apples with a blush of red at the stem. Some of the trees in the dooryards carry old grapevines, thicker than a man's arm.

During the eighteenth century, the predominant tree on the Moun-

Julie Polhemus measures the Prestons' maple tree.

tain was the American chestnut. It figured as a corner marker in almost every deed. Chestnut was the lumber of choice for home building, barns, and furniture. But the blight carried off the chestnut tree. Today, saplings spring from soil where an ancestor tree rotted but the young chestnuts all die before maturity.[2]

People rarely visit the wood and hills of Preston Mountain. During the fall, a few hunters seek game birds, turkeys, and deer. They rarely venture far from the roads. Few people are lucky enough to see the wildest inhabitants. In 1700, the Mountain was home to wolves, panthers, and every other native wild beast. Wolves and panthers may be the only such beasts that have not come back. Wildcat and deer, which had probably disappeared by 1900, mounted a comeback in the 1930s. Since then, the beaver, wild turkey, coyote, otter, raven, and black bear have returned.

One creature never left. From the time of first settlement, a thriving population of rattlesnakes made Preston Mountain notorious. At one time, herpetologists collected rattlers on the Mountain. Settlers located snake dens and mounted forays to massacre the reptiles. The den sites are kept secret now to protect the endangered rattlesnakes.[3]

Though it is barely seventy-five miles north of Manhattan, Preston Mountain seems as wild as the Catskills or the Adironadacks. While the animals have come back, the human community founded there in the 1700s has disappeared. Preston Mountain is a ghost town.

Chapter Two
"A Mighty Hunter"

ON A SPRING MORNING IN 1766, MARTIN PRESTON, his wife Rebecca, and their three young sons started up the road from Kent to "the Hoveout," a mountainous tract west of Kent in New York colony. Perhaps Rebecca rode the plow horse with the infant Obadiah in her arms. Martin walked behind the oxen with a whip in his hand. The oxen pulled a two-wheeled cart piled high with the family's belongings. Five-year-old Timothy and two-year-old David squeezed into the cart.

The journey climaxed years of planning and preparation. They climbed the road to their new home in New York. The road was no more than a rough cart path that angled up the steep north side of Mount Algo. It began gradually enough just west of the crossing of Macedonia Brook, but then it turned uphill and climbed steeply beside another brook. Once the Prestons entered the forest, their sense of leaving home and roots must have grown stronger. It would take most of the day for them to reach their new home. Though it was only four miles from Kent, it was remote and crude. They would lead different lives than before.

Martin and Rebecca had married in Kent on New Years Day in 1761, when he was twenty and she was seventeen. Rebecca was the eldest of the five children of Philip Judd, one of the original proprietors of Kent. Though Philip owned property, he also had a young family to support. By 1766, the shares of the proprietors had been divided and redivided, limiting opportunities for younger people. Rebecca's dower, if any, was small. Nor could Martin Preston look forward to inheriting property on his side. His father, David Preston, died when Martin was fourteen. His mother, Elizabeth, quickly married Daniel Brownson in Kent in 1756. Daniel's first wife had died less than six months before. Marriage was more than romance in the eighteenth century—it was an economic necessity.[1]

A young family needed land. Martin and Rebecca Preston would have to provide their own portion in life. They chose to move to new land. The homesite they selected lay on the western ridge of the Mountain, overlooking the valley of the TenMile River to the west. They built their home beside a path at the south end of a high hill. Mortmeadow Brook flowed west past their front door; their house faced the brook, not the path. After the land was cleared there would be a fine view down the Mountain and across the valley. The west wind swept the site; at twelve hundred feet in the air it could be a frightening place in a thunderstorm, but it was sheltered from the north winds of winter.[2]

The ruins of Martin and Rebecca Preston's house.

Martin built a two-story home with a central chimney of stone and big fireplaces on both floors. He cut trees and adzed them square for the frame. He probably carted logs to a sawmill in Kent or Webatuck to be sawn into boards. He needed help from friends or relatives to raise the chimney and the timber frame. Most of the timbers in the new house were probably hewn from American chestnut trees. These giant trees made up "more than a quarter of eastern woodlands." The native chestnuts in the eighteenth century stood one hundred feet tall with trunks five feet in diameter.[3]

Preston cleared an acre around the house and planted a few apple trees. North of the house, along the cart path, a meadow emerged from the smoking stumps and piles of stone. In time he would build a barn across the road near the stream. There

Martin Preston's dam today.

would be a bridge across the stream in front of the house. He kept beehives nearby. One day he would be locally famous as a maker of a mead called "metheglin," made from his own honey and laced with other spirits.

Martin dammed the brook across the road from the house. The dam was a structure of massive stone, thirty feet long by eight feet high. Probably, he intended to run a sawmill there, as there was sufficient water for livestock nearby. If so, the remnants of the sawmill have disappeared, but the large dam remains.

Rebecca lived a lonely life. She kept house, cooked, looked after the children, and relied on herself. It was an all-day trip to visit her parents, virtually impossible with three little boys. Her nearest neighbors were strangers down in the valley, many of them Dutch people whose broken English she could barely understand. If Martin or one of the boys became ill or injured, Rebecca was the only nurse, doctor, or minister they would ever see. Such a life could make or break a woman's spirit. Apparently, Rebecca did not break. She would live in that house another sixty-two years, bear eight more children, bury three of them in the cemetery on the hill across the brook, and be surrounded in her old age by children, grandchildren, and great-grandchildren.

Martin, too, faced tests of his self-reliance. A crop must be planted, raised, and harvested before winter. Food for humans and animals alike came from their land. He likely sowed winter rye while he was clearing the land, casting it by handfuls on the raw earth among the stumps, along with buckwheat to shade out the weeds. The hay crop was a mixture of clover and brome; it was a small crop because it took years to dig and stone a hay meadow. He grew Indian corn for cattle and people, and oats for the horse. In a large garden they grew squash, potatoes, and beans. Martin needed to select and preserve seeds from each variety he planted for the next year. There was no room for error here.

He set out a small orchard of apple trees on the north-facing hill along the road to Kent. In years to come, that hill would be the best plow land on the farm. The last glacier had scoured it of boulders, leaving instead a soil of fine gravelly loam. After Martin and his growing sons had cleared the field on the hill, they walled off a half-acre for a public cemetery.

Like his wife, Martin had family nearby. His older brother, Ebenezer, operated gristmills along the TenMile River at Webatuck, five miles south of Martin's homestead. Ebenezer was thirteen years older than his brother, and already he was a prosperous man. His neighbors called him "Captain" Preston, an honorific title bestowed for practical success, not military rank. Perhaps Ebenezer taught Martin the art of water-driven mills; Martin would later own a sawmill with his son. There is no evidence, however, that the two brothers were close.[4]

Martin's sister Sarah was probably close to him, though she was twelve years older. She married Joshua Agard when Martin was eight years old. Her children, Joseph, James, and Sarah, were only a few years younger than Martin. Two of them, James and Sarah (married name Philleo or Fillow) eventually settled on the Mountain. With their children coming on, the settlement on the Mountain began to take on the character of a clan.

The Preston family genealogy claimed that "Martin was a mighty hunter; sometimes on his hunting expositions he would go as far as the Catskill Mountains." Those must have been prodigious hunting trips, lasting many days, and involving ferrying horses and hunters across the Hudson. Certainly, he hunted in the mountains around his home. He owned a "fowling piece," and there were geese and ducks in the swamps nearby. Among his effects after his death was "one old French gun," origin unknown.[5]

The Schaghticoke (or Scatacook, as it was then spelled) Indians may have been troubled by the Preston's homestead on the Mountain. These Native Americans had occupied the southeastern slopes of the Mountain for many years, perhaps many generations. In 1752, the General Assembly of Connecticut set aside land for the Schaghticokes in Kent, bounded by the Housatonic River on the east and the New York line on the west. Seen on a modern topographic map, those lands would extend from near Bull's Bridge at the south end to Thayer Brook, just north of Chapel Pond. Even so, the Indians were accustomed to thinking of the entire Mountain as their ancestral hunting grounds. There is anecdotal evidence that hunting parties of Indians and colonists encountered one another in the forests of Preston Mountain. These encounters discouraged and embittered the Indians. But there were no reports of violence.[6]

The 1760s were crucial years in the history of Anglo-Indian relations in the new world. The French and Indian War (or "the Old French War" as the colonists called it) ended in 1763, after a dozen years of hostilities. Much of the fighting took place in the wilderness of northern New York. One enduring consequence of the war, for both colonists and Indians alike, was their collective memory of its brutality. No person then alive had ever experienced the vicious acts and mutual hatred that colored this war. Scalping and mutilation of captives were common on both sides. In 1757, as the French general Montcalm prepared to lay siege to Fort William Henry on Lake George, his Indian allies took English prisoners. They boiled them and ate them in sight of other prisoners waiting their turn.[7]

During the war, fear of such atrocities reached as far south as Kent and Dover. In nearby Sharon, it was reported:

> The Old French War was commenced about this time [1750] and the stories of indian atrocities which were borne on every breeze, filled the whole country with terror and alarm. Four persons were murdered about this time between Stockbridge and Lenox, and this, with other alarming incidents, produced a very general consternation in Sharon.[8]

The general consternation also brought consequences to Sharon: "One John Palmer testified that he shot a lurking indian in Sharon in 1754, thinks he broke his right arm, heard the indian whoop."[9]

The Old French War sowed seeds of hatred and fear that bore fruit for many years. On Preston Mountain and in the surrounding towns, the war marked the beginning of generations of mutual distrust among the races.

The distrust is all the more ironic because the Schaghticokes consistently fought on the side of the colonists in every conflict. One of them, Warrop Chickens, served with Colonel Nathan Whiting's 2nd Regiment of Connecticut Militia. This regiment fought in a famous skirmish with the enemy, known afterward as "the bloody morning scout." French soldiers and Indian warriors ambushed Whiting and his British allies early one morning at the Drowned Lands, southeast of Lake George. The English side fared badly until Whiting took command of a retreat. The bodies of the slain were mutilated and thrown into "Bloody Pond."[10]

Chickens' loyalty to the colonial side was not repaid well. Forty years later, his grandson Benjamin Chickens would suffer a loss on the Mountain—a loss that involved the Preston family. We examine his fate in Chapter Ten.

Another colonist with ties to Preston Mountain served with Whiting's regiment. Roswell Dart, a carpenter, signed a petition in 1786 asking the New York government to recognize his claims to land on the

Mountain. Forty men signed this petition, including Martin Preston and two of his sons. But there is no proof that Dart ever lived on the Mountain. He would have made a colorful neighbor, for he led an adventurous life. He enlisted to fight again in 1776, as a minuteman. The muster rolls describe him as five feet, ten inches tall, with a "fresh complexion, gray eyes and black hair."[11]

Roswell may have been running from trouble when he enlisted the second time. In January 1775, Justice Andrew Morhaus of Pawlingstown charged him with "aiding and abetting in taking away Mary the wife of George Harrington and in assaulting and attempting to break open said Harrington's house in the deadtime of night. . . ."[12] Justice Morhaus left no record of the disposition of the case. Since Dart remained in the area for several more years, it is likely that Mary was the subject of a practical joke (perhaps the result of too much rum), and not the victim of a serious kidnapping.[12]

Martin Preston's name does not appear on the rolls of men who served in the French and Indian War. He was the right age to serve, and he was certainly sufficiently vigorous enough to be a soldier. Except for the service he gave to his large extended family on the Mountain, he seems to have lived out his life without becoming involved in any of the conflicts that boiled up around him. His sons followed his example.

By the autumn of 1766, Martin harvested his first crop on the new farm. He probably slaughtered a hog in the yard on a frosty evening for bacon and ham and salt pork. Chickens roamed the barnyard, prey for foxes. Called "dunghill fowl" to reflect their eating habits, they provided meat and eggs. If there was a fresh cow for milk, she would need a bull the next year to maintain her in milk. Stallions, bulls, rams, and boars—all male beasts—though essential, added greatly to the difficulty and danger of farming for Martin, and even more, for his children.

Rebecca's three boys required all her vigilance. She had to concentrate on weighing hazards; an infant, a toddler, and a curious boy of five found them all. Whether it was the open flame in the hearth, the axe and saw in the woodshed, the loaded gun over the mantel, or the open well in the yard, her home contained many threats to the children. She carried this burden by herself. Perhaps her younger sister, Annah Judd, age twelve, came to visit. Annah was old enough to watch the baby and to keep the boys occupied. Later, she would marry Martin's nephew, James Agard. Together, they settled a homestead on the Mountain a mile south of Martin and Rebecca.

When the weather turned cold, one of Rebecca's chief worries was the fire—it must never go out. The open flame provided all the heat for the home. If it went out they might freeze or be unable to eat. Flint and steel worked well enough for dry tinder, but on a windy, snowy night the kindling might not ignite.

The first winter on the Mountain presented a stern test. Martin spent his days in the woods felling timber, alone. To stay alive he had to drop the trees accurately and get out of the way when they fell. The oxen hauled logs on icy trails with Martin alongside, where a slip could mean a broken leg or worse.

Still, there must have been a sweetness to this hard life. Each day the clearing around their home grew a bit. They could see smoke from the chimneys in the valley. It was brighter on sunny days. There was the constant aroma of new-sawn timber; the sappy smell permeated every board of the house and every stump and brush pile outside. The scent of wood smoke was also constant. There were baskets of potatoes in the cellar (or "in the hole," as the pioneers said), and sacks of corn and rye.

The excitement of living in a new home must have been a tonic to them. They faced lives with more freedom and more opportunity than any of their ancestors could have dreamed. But, in 1766, they had no way to know this. They were descendants of the old colonial order in which a man's place in the world was preordained by the condition of his birth, and a woman's place was subservient to all. Most of all, their happiness must have been tempered by the nagging awareness that they did not own, nor have any legal right to, the land they lived on.

The Puritan Prestons of Salem

LIKE ALL PEOPLE, Martin Preston grew up with family behind him; and he learned family stories and traditions to instruct and sustain him. Eighteenth century families existed without electronic entertainment or communications. Families amused themselves by talking to each other. It was all the education that most people received. The family story that Martin learned would be a warning to any man.

His great-great-grandfather Roger Preston set sail from England to Boston on a ship called the *Elizabeth of London, William Stagg, Master* on April 8, 1635. Roger joined the Puritan colony in Massachusetts, first settling at Ipswich, then moving to Salem in 1660. At age forty-six, he started a new occupation at Salem, keeping an ordinary or tavern. In September 1660, the court at Salem granted him a license: "Roger Preston is allowed by this court to keep an ordinary and to sell strong liquors for ye entertainment of strangers for ye year ensuing." Perhaps Roger's recipe for metheglin made Martin famous.[13]

Roger's wife, Martha, bore him seven children: Thomas, Mary, Elizabeth, Samuel, John, Jacob, and Levi. It was the second generation of American Prestons who lived through Salem's years of fire and brimstone. They had suffered the death of their father in January 1666 and the prompt remarriage of their mother to Nicholas Holt in May of the same year.

John and Samuel (who was Martin's great-grandfather) were teenagers when their father died. Their stepfather (with their mother's consent) wasted no time in apprenticing them out. It was indentured servitude; they lived completely dependent upon the generosity and kindness of their masters (though apprenticeship was nominally a contractual arrangement). Samuel apparently fared well, for he became a carpenter and farmer.

Younger brother Jacob was not so lucky. At age thirteen he was apprenticed to a blacksmith, Thomas Chandler of Merrimack. Chandler sold Jacob to William Curtis of Salem. Jacob refused to stay with Curtis, although the local court ordered him to stay. He ran away to sea and never returned. When his estate was settled in court, the judge wrote:

> Jacob Preston whoe in all probabilitie hath been departed this life for these several months having bin wanting about nine or ten months gone forth in a small ketch upon a fishing design to the eastward & never yet returned nor certainly heard of. [14]

Jacob's estate assets consisted of his clothing, worth seven pounds, which just paid his debts.

Roger's eldest son, Thomas, initiated the Preston's connection with the Salem witch trials. His wife was Rebecca Nurse, daughter of the famous Rebecca Nurse who was hanged as a witch in 1692 and made immortal as the saintly old woman in Arthur Miller's play, *The Crucible*. Rebecca Preston tried in vain to save her mother's life by signing a petition on her mother's behalf:

> We whose nams are under written: can testifie if cald to it that goode nurse have bene trobled with an infirmity of body for many years which the juree of women seme to be Afraid it should be something else. [15]

Rebecca's husband, Thomas Preston, differed from his wife. He was one of the several Salem yeomen who swore to warrants, complaining of alleged witches. He signed a warrant against the impoverished Salem women, Sarah Good and Sarah Osborne, and he signed one against Reverend Parris's slave, Tituba. Both Parris and Tituba became prominent characters in *The Crucible*. Sarah Goode was executed.

Thomas's younger brother John Preston was one of the brave citizens who signed a petition in favor of the accused. One of those he supported was Sarah Wilson Sr., who was Martin Preston's great-grandmother.

Martin's great-grandfather Samuel represented the schism in

the Preston family during these frightful times. His petition accusing Martha Carrier betrays the madness of the period:

> Samuel Preston, aged about 41 years Saith that about 3 years since I had some difference with Martha Carrier w'ch also had happened sever'll times before and soon after I lost a Cow in a strange manner begin cast upon her back w'th her heels up in firm ground when she was very lusty it being June & within abo't month after this the s'd Martha & I had some difference again at which Time she told me I had lost a Cow lately & it Would not or should not be long before I should loose Another w'ch accordingly came to pass for i had a Cow that was well kept with English hay & I could not p'ceive that she aild any thing & yet she pined & quickly lay downe as if she was asleep & dyed.[16]

Samuel's son Jacob was eleven when his father "cried out" Martha Carrier. Ten years after the 1692 witch persecutions, Jacob married Sarah Wilson, daughter of Sarah and Joseph Wilson. Sarah, the mother, and Sarah, the daughter, (known at the trials as Sarah Wilson Sr. and Sarah Wilson Jr.) were both charged with witchcraft. Jacob's future bride, then only thirteen, saved her life by confessing. On September 16, 1692, she joined a handful of girls in admitting their collusion with the devil, alleging that Abigail Faulkner of Andover led her "into the dradful sin of witchcraft."

The relatively small number of people scorched by the witchcraft craze must have created a sort of league or society. Perhaps others shunned them; maybe they sought each other out for some reason, for Jacob and Sarah's son David married Elizabeth Martin, great-granddaughter of Susannah Martin, hanged as a witch beside Rebecca Nurse. Susannah was the widow of George Martin of Amesbury. Many people accused her, but she was brave and defiant when examined. She laughed upon entering the court; when the judge asked her why, she answered, "Well I may at such folly." She refused to confess, telling the court, "I dare not tell a lye to save my life."[17]

Not surprisingly, the Prestons left Salem quickly, and they kept moving. Samuel moved to Andover. His son Jacob moved to Windham, Connecticut, with his large family, including Martin's father, David. David, for his turn, moved to the Oblong about 1747. With him was seven-year-old Martin, named for his mother's family.[13]

It was characteristic of Martin and his sons that they joined nothing. None of them fought in the wars of the eighteenth century. Their names were absent from the militia rolls and the annals of the Anti-Rent Rebellion. Nor did a Preston from the Mountain join a church. They worked hard and minded their own business—a safe practice for folks from Salem.

Chapter Three
The Oblong and "The Hoveout Lands"

MARTIN PRESTON NEVER RECORDED A DEED for his land on Preston Mountain. A survey map of his land, prepared late in his life, revealed that he owned 645 acres, 3 rods, and 22 perches of land—more than a square mile of the Mountain. Whatever the basis of his claim to this domain, it was never a document of public record.[1]

In fact, none of the original settlers of the Mountain ever recorded a deed. A dozen or more pioneers settled there. They cleared the land, fenced it, cultivated it, built homes, and there, lived out their lives. When they died, their heirs inherited the farms. Occasionally, the second generation sold their parents' land, conveying the places by deeds with surveyed descriptions; and these later deeds were usually recorded. The first deed ever recorded for a Preston Mountain settler was in 1801, and the buyer was an African American man, whose story is told in Chapter Eight.[2]

A recorded deed lent reliability to the claim of ownership of the possessor of the land. That was the purpose of the recording statutes: they "settled" claims of title based upon the first recorded deed. Some colonists may have been ignorant of the recording laws. They kept their deeds in drawers where a mouse or a fire could destroy all proof of their title.

If Preston was ignorant of the need to record his deed in 1766, he knew better by 1788. In the latter year, he purchased ninety acres in Kent from Nathan Hoyt, and he promptly recorded his deed in the Kent land records. However, despite his awareness of the practice, he still never recorded a deed for his real estate on Preston Mountain. It is likely that he never had such a deed, nor did any of his neighbors. They would not have known from whom to obtain the land. Preston Mountain was the center of a confusing title controversy that had been going on since the 1600s.[3]

The boundary between the colonies of New York and Connecticut was uncertain until well into the eighteenth century. At the time, its location was unimportant. Wherever the line ran in 1650, it was way out in the wilderness. Nobody cared. New York's Dutch settlements hugged the coast and the Hudson River. Connecticut's population, too, stayed near Long Island Sound and the Connecticut River. Their common boundary passed through rugged mountains and forest, not yet of concern to either colony.

In the early eighteenth century, however, settlements in the two colonies began to approach each other. By 1707, English settlers had moved up the Housatonic River to the site of New Milford, a few miles south of the Mountain. In 1711, Richard Sackett lived on a tract just north of the Mountain near the site of Wassaic. Sackett was the first to refer to the area as "Dover." In the 1728 Dutchess County tax lists, several Dutch families appear for the first time in Dover: Derick DeDuyster, Jacob Van Campen, and Arie Rosa, all members of the Kingston Dutch Reformed Church. Two years later, Jan Oosterhuit joined them. These Dutchmen were getting close to the English moving in from Connecticut.

The tendency of the English and Dutch settlers to move closer to each other existed the entire length of the border, from the Sound to Massachusetts. Connecticut citizens, in fact, had already moved into places nominally in New York: the present towns of Stanford, Greenwich, and New Canaan. New York agreed to cede these lands to Connecticut in exchange for an "Equivalent" amount of land. It was proposed that the "Equivalent land" would be a long, narrow strip along the presumed border. From its shape on a map this land would acquire the name, "the Oblong."[4]

Before the deal could be closed, New York needed to resolve claims to the new land that some of its most powerful citizens had raised. Unlike the New England colonies, great families and wealthy patent holders, not farmers and smallholders, owned most of New

York. From Westchester County north to Albany, a de facto aristocracy owned large patents and manors east of the Hudson, and they controlled their holdings like medieval baronies. The families of Van Cortlandt, Phillipse, Beekman, Livingston, and Schuyler dominated over one hundred miles of the borderlands, and leased it to "tenants." These landlords expected that the "Oblong" would be attached to their manors.[5]

As the beneficiaries of a long tradition of government corruption, these families were used to getting what they wanted. For almost a century, the English governors of New York made a business of granting vast amounts of land to favored clients; most of these grants were illegal or fraudulent.

> The seeds of social discontent were sown deeply in the system of colonial land distribution. On the eve of the Revolution, an inequitable distribution of great landed wealth acquired at slight cost by shrewd landlords provoked the wrath of small farmers. The circumstances under which this land was acquired must have added to the bitterness of the yeoman's envy. For discerning eyes could catch glimpses of transactions that were not without taint of fraud. Huge grants were inspired by bribes, family connections, and fee hunger. Colonial governors made many of these illegal sales in violation of colonial statutes or British instructions, which limited the size, or prohibited the making, of land grants.[6]

Where outright grants could not be made to individuals, "dummies," or fictitious parties, accepted the grants. "Where these limitations on the transfer of land were not boldly violated, they were subtly circumvented by the use of 'dummy' grantees or of fictitious names."[7]

Several government officials would figure prominently in the Oblong problem. One was Lieutenant Governor George Clarke, who held office from 1736 to 1743 and who "acquired over 100,000 acres through the use of dummy partners."[8]

Cadwallader Colden was Surveyor General of New York when the Oblong question was settled. He was widely regarded as one of the most accomplished men in America. He understood the consequences of New York's corrupt land practices. In 1732, he wrote:

And every year the young people go from this Province and Purchase Land in the Neighboring Colonies, while much better and
every way more convenient lands lie useless to the King and Country. The reason for this is that the Grantees themselves are not, nor
ever were in a capacity to improve such large Tracts and other people will not become their Vassals or Tenants for one great reason—
leaving their native Country, was to avoid dependence on landlords,
and to enjoy in fee to descend to their posterity that their children
may reap the benefit of their labor and Industry.[9]

But Colden himself, if he never took bribes, enjoyed the fees paid
to him upon the continual transfer of lands to the aristocracy. He puz-
zled to resolve the question of future ownership of the Oblong. He
hoped to forestall the greed of the large landowners by appealing to
their interests as merchants. Settlement of the Oblong would greatly
increase the market for goods produced by the manors. Still, Colden
could conceive of no way to pay the cost of surveying the vast tract.
While most Crown grants were purposely vague (allowing the
grantees license to grab more land than was intended), it was in New
York's best interest to be precise about the Oblong.[10]

Finally, George Clarke proposed forming a company of investors
to pay the survey costs. In return, the investors would receive grants
in the Oblong. Colden agreed. New York lawyers and power brokers
James Alexander, Archibald Kennedy, William Smith, James Brown,
and many others became investors. They named their enterprise Hawley and Company.[11]

With financial backing in place, surveyors began mapping the
Oblong. They crisscrossed the forests from Westchester County to
Massachusetts, measuring with chains and compasses. They located
the new border between Connecticut and New York one and four-
fifths miles east of the old one. Their assistants built stone cairns,
called "monuments," at every even-numbered mile counting from the
southerly end on both the old and the new colony lines. One day they
stood on the old line at the westernmost ridge of Preston Mountain.
Their report for the day stated:

At the distance of thirty miles as aforesaid in said line we sett up a
stake and heaped up some stone round it for a Monument on the

West side of a Mountain being about south East from the House of Yacob van Campons and Derrick Dutcheers. . . .[12]

One of the Oblong surveyors was a Quaker man named Nathan Birdsall. In the course of his work, Birdsall looked for likely land for his own farm. He found it on the hill immediately south of Preston Mountain. He and his wife, Jane, later became some of the first settlers on "Quaker Hill" in Pawling, New York. He would lead a movement of the Society of Friends to this new place. Their daughter Sarah married another Quaker surveyor, Nathan Soule. Soule played a role several times in the history of Preston Mountain.

After the Oblong was surveyed, representatives of the two colonies signed an agreement at Dover confirming the location of the new boundary, called by McCracken, "The Treaty of Dover. " The signing took place on May 14, 1731. The next day, in London, England, the king's representatives in council:

> granted to Chandos' dummies, Sir Thomas Eyles & Co., the entire 64,000 acres of the patent (the Oblong). In New York, all unaware, Rip Van Dam for the Governor in Council executed the deed to Thomas Hawley & Co. on June 8, for their 50,000.[13]

These two separate grants for the same land touched off twenty years of litigation in the New York chancery courts. The dual grants propagated doubts about land titles in the Oblong that persisted for much longer than twenty years. Eventually, Chandos lost the Thomas Eyles and Company claim, but persons claiming title through Chandos and Eyles continued to appear until the Revolution settled all questions.

There was a critical difference between the Chandos and Hawley grants. Eleven thousand four hundred acres was left out of the Hawley and Company grant. Though part of the Oblong, this land was considered too rough and worthless to be of any value. It was "hove out" of the grant. It became known as the "Hoveout Land."[14]

Regardless of conflicting claims, Hawley and Company promptly set out to divide the Oblong into "lotts" of five hundred acres each. These lotts, almost square in dimension, were laid out two abreast and numbered from south to north, one through eighty.

South of Preston Mountain were Lotts 43 and 44. Lott 44 was set off to George Clarke. Lott 43 included Lake Ellis. North of the Mountain, Cadwallader Colden acquired Lott 45 near the modern hamlet of South Amenia. Lott 46, including parts of Peaked Mountain and Bog Hollow, was conveyed to the children of William Burnett, Esquire. Between these numbered lotts stretched seven miles of blank space on the map—Preston Mountain was the largest portion of the Hoveout Land.[15]

Before long, men saw value in the empty space. On April 4, 1750, Samuel Rogers and Anthony Tancret petitioned the colony government for twenty-five hundred acres at the north end of the Hoveout tract. This acreage extended south from Lotts 45 and 46 to the south end of what is today Crane Pond. A deed dated December 1750 conveyed three thousand acres to Tancret and Rogers. Governor Clinton, Archibald Kennedy as collector and receiver general, George Clarke Jr. as secretary of the province, and Cadwallader Colden as surveyor general of the province—all partners in Hawley and Company—signed it. They conveyed the parcel in their official capacity, not as Hawley and Company partners.[16]

It is unclear whether Tancret and Rogers acquired the land for their own benefit. To discourage corruption, a colonial law limited the land that could be granted any one individual. Perhaps Tancret and Rogers were dummies for more substantial men, like the grantors on their deed.

Though the grant was made to "Anthony" Tancret, "Antoine" Tancret signed the petition for the grant. Antoine arrived in America from France in about 1725. He married here and fathered four children—three sons and a daughter. All three sons served on the American side in the Revolution. Tancret lived in Northeast Precinct (now the town of Northeast) from 1754 to 1779.[17]

Tancret and Rogers sold a large parcel of their land to another Frenchman, Dr. Benjamin Delavergne. The doctor built a dam on the brook that flows south through Bog Hollow. He was known to his neighbors as "the French doctor," and his dam, "the French doctor's dam." Delavergne "played a prominent part in the beginning of the Revolution, and was Major in the Fourth Regiment of Dutchess County Militia."[18] The French doctor's lands appear as adjoining parcels in several later Preston Mountain deeds.

Settlers inhabited the Mountain as early as the 1750s, but they did not remain, and most of their names are lost. Henry Noble McCracken wrote in his history of Dutchess County, *Old Dutchess Forever*, "These [rocky hillsides] soon became known as 'The Hoveout Lands', and as such became the residence of squatters and penniless tenants who sometimes asked for the crumbs from the master's table." McCracken identified neither the squatters, the masters, nor the source for his assertion. Nevertheless, it is true that poor people gravitated to the Hoveout and Preston Mountain, and some of them appealed to the Crown's agents for help. In 1752, William Kempe was attorney general of New York when he learned that Hawley and Company was evicting squatters from the Hoveout Lands.

> Residents of Hoveout Mountain Land, threatened with eviction, appealed to Kempe for protection. The attorney examined the records, and scenting a chance at lucrative litigation, he revived the Chandos suit. He did more; he issued a proclamation demanding that all residents of the Oblong apply for licenses under the Chandos Patent. A few something over a score of the farmers were scared into applying, thus giving him a cause to plead.[19]

This was a case of the rich and powerful taking advantage of the weak. The partners of Hawley and Company, who sought to evict the squatters, had no more right to the land than those they dispossessed—the Hoveout Lands had not been included in the Hawley and Company grant. William Kempe explained matters in a letter to a Mr. Farquaharson in England:

> There were formerly some families of poor people that had settled on some of the fruitful spots of the Equivalent land the title of the English patentees [Chandos]. These the New York patentees [Hawley and Company] drove off by violence, and then many of them went and settled on here and there a spot which they picked out of the Best of these Hoveout Lands, expecting they should there have been quiet, as the New York patentees had then no claim to these Lands. But since their modern patent, they have endeavoured to dispossess them there likewise and have drove off many of them.[20]

It is unclear what Kempe meant by "modern patent." Had Hawley and Company acquired the Hoveout Lands by some other means? Two partners would later claim some of the Hoveout this way. But no grant to Hawley and Company exists for the whole tract. Kempe vowed to take up the cause of the poor squatters, which, of course, was also the cause of Chandos against the partners of Hawley and Company. Apparently, Kempe failed to interest the English patentees in reviving the Chandos suit (which would have been his only source for a fee because the squatters couldn't pay him). He never followed through on his vow.

In 1752, the two Hawley partners, William Smith and James Brown, petitioned Governor George Clinton for four parcels in the Hoveout Lands, two of which were on Preston Mountain. They recited their reasons for requesting the lands:

> That in order to obtain the said grant [the Oblong in 1731] your Petitioners had born a considerable part of a very great and unusual expense in running the Division Lines between the two Colonies. . . .
>
> That pursuant to [illegible] this Government your Petitioners had also born a considerable part of the expenses of the Purchase from the Native Indians of about Eleven thousand Acres of Land [the Hoveout Lands] not included or granted by the said Letters Patent which purchase was made and the Consideration thereof paid by your Petitioner James Brown as by Deeds in the hands of your Petitioners might appear. . . .
>
> That the said Eleven thousand Acres of Land were Not Esteemed at the Time of obtaining the said patent worth the Annual Rent and the Patent Charges.[21]

It cannot be said that no such conveyance was ever made. It may be that the petition refers to the "modern patent" that Kempe alluded to. It is a fact that the public records contain no conveyance of the Hoveout Lands to Hawley and Company. Also, Smith and Brown did not seek the whole of the Hoveout—just parcels in it. The 1752 petition raises several important questions, but answers none of them.

First, the assertion that Brown had purchased the eleven thousand acres from the Indians is unique. No history or account of colonial New York claims that colonists purchased any part of the Oblong from the Indians, and Connecticut histories do not relate that the Schaghti-cokes sold or deeded any portion of the Mountain to white men. In 1752 Connecticut set aside the land in Kent for the benefit of the Indi-ans, and it is not impossible that the Schaghticokes gave up their claims in New York at the same time. Smith and Brown's petition alone supports that proposition.[22]

Second, what became of the "Deeds in the hands of your Petition-ers?" The implication was that Brown purchased the land from the Indi-ans as an agent for others, not for his own account. Why else allege that he and Smith paid "part of the expense?" Apparently, they kept the deeds, which have not since surfaced.

Third, what attracted the petitioners to the particular parcels they sought? Two of the parcels were on Preston Mountain. One was locat-ed on the southwest flank of the Mountain, just north of Lake Ellis. It consisted of steep, rocky hillside, fully deserving of the name "Hoveout Land." The other parcel, however, was six hundred acres located due east of the thirty-mile monument on the old colony line. It was the best of the land on the Mountain; in future years this parcel would be the core of the community on Preston Mountain. Perhaps someone acting for Smith and Brown examined the site and identified it as a promising spot in the forest. More likely, someone else had already commenced improving this land, cleared part of the forest, started crops, and squat-ted there. Whatever the condition of the six hundred acres in 1752, its boundaries are strikingly similar to the limits of a core of farms culti-vated there fifty years later, including the farms of Martin Preston and his sons.[23]

The 1752 petition found a willing reader in Governor Clinton or his council, because Cadwallader Colden caused a survey map of the parcels to be made, and they appear on one of Colden's maps of the Oblong. But no grant of the parcels to Smith and Brown was ever recorded. If squatters lived on one or both parcels, they may have been evicted. The best evidence shows that some of these people, or their chil-dren, returned to the Mountain.

The Beekman Precinct tax lists from the 1740s and 1750s contain the surnames of families that later settled on Preston Mountain. Joshua Agard and John Cummins were taxed in the Oblong, though the exact

Cadwallader Colden

CADWALLADER COLDEN was one of the ablest and most interesting of the Crown's agents in the New World. Michael Kammen's work, *Colonial New York: A History*, says of him:

> The most systematic inquiries into science and philosophy were undertaken by Cadwallader Colden, who had studied at Edinburgh and London, practiced medicine in Pennsylvania, and published his first scientific work, Animal Secretions, in 1715 at the age of twenty-seven. He came to New York in 1718, immersed himself in administrative affairs and politics, but also found time later on to write treatises on botanical topics, disease, gravitation, calculus and philosophy. He corresponded with eminent European scientists and introduced the Linnaean system of classification to America (1742-44) soon after its original publication in 1737.[24]

Colden and Benjamin Franklin corresponded for many years, though Franklin makes no mention of him in his autobiography. Colden was a true son of the enlightenment, and colonial New York must have seemed a rude immersion in chaos. In various government offices, he struggled to bring rationality and honesty to the administration. But the colonies were struggling in the opposite direction, striving to throw off order. Even Colden's small prize, Lott 45 in the Oblong just north of Preston Mountain, brought him surprising trouble.

Lott 45 rested athwart an earlier claim of title made by Richard Sackett. Sackett had settled on his claim near present-day Wassaic in 1711. Though his title was tenuous, Sackett attempted to perfect it by possession. At his death, he passed the land on to his son John Sackett, whose claim conflicted with Colden's. After the Oblong division, Colden leased part of Lott 45 to Thomas Wolcott. This parcel was along the Webatuck Creek at South Amenia. Thomas ran a mill there. Later, his son Luke played a prominent role in local history. He also married Abigail Preston, Martin and Rebecca's daughter. But, in 1749, Thomas Wolcott struggled to gain a foothold as a tenant on Colden's land.

On August 24, 1749, Cadwallader Colden wrote to John Crook and described Woolcott's problem:

> One Thomas Woolcott a Tenant I have on a lott of land in the Oblong near Dover in Dutchess county tells me that while he was raising a logg house on that land & had it as high as to be ready to lay the wallplaits John Sackett towards evening came with an ax in his hand & while Woolcott was upon the house he began with his Ax to cut the timber to pieces on which Woolcott came down & pull'd him from the house & some struggle happen'd afterwards between them. About a week afterwards Woolcott on the complaint of John Sackett was taken into Custody & carried by Warrant from Justice Barton of Filkingtone before him. . . .[25]

Years of litigation ensued between Sackett and Cadwallader Colden. Meanwhile, in 1754, Thomas Woolcott married John Sackett's daughter, Catherine. Together, they had seven children, including Luke who was born in 1755. Either Thomas patched up his squabble with his future father-in-law, or the squabble was a sham to begin with. If Colden knew of his tenant's marriage, he must have been scratching his head.

Colden went on to be lieutenant governor and governor of the colony of New York. In 1765, the Stamp Act precipitated a riot in New York City, and a mob forced him to take refuge on a British warship. Later, another mob burned his coach with his effigy inside. Colden died in 1776 as the ultimate chaos of the Revolution descended on his colony.[26]

location of their homes is unknown. Their sons, James Agard and Simeon Cummins, did live on the Mountain. The fathers may have been among those who were evicted.

One early settler on the Hoveout left a record of his claim of title for his farm. The 1786 petition of Benjamin Benson narrated the history of ninety-seven acres on the very top of the Mountain adjacent to the Connecticut line and the Schagticoke Reservation. Benson attested that, in 1751, Benjamin Pearce possessed the farm. Pearce sold it to Mathias Marsh and William Marsh in 1760 or 1761, and they in turn conveyed it to Benjamin Benson in 1764. In 1766, Benjamin's brother Ambrose Benson possessed the farm, having paid his brother to convey it to Heziah Benson, Ambrose's daughter. Ambrose held the land under his daughter's title, even after she married James Morhouse. A family dispute commenced over the mountaintop homestead.[27]

Several neighbors sided with Ambrose; they filed affidavits claiming that Ambrose was the real occupant. John Bull, a miller at nearby Bull's Bridge, confirmed the claim. While William Payne and Nathan Soule surveyed the colony line, Ambrose's daughter Mary Benson warned them off the land, according to Payne's affidavit. Another surveyor, Phineas Lewis, swore that he, Nathan Soule, and Jedediah Hubble were forbidden by Mary Benson from "crossing the meadow in the name of James Morhouse at first and then afterward of her father" (Ambrose Benson). Apparently, James Morhouse claimed the land as dower from his marriage to Heziah. As with many title disputes of the period, the question of possession assumed paramount importance.[28]

The documents establish that, as early as 1751, Benjamin Pearce had cleared land, built a home, and set out an orchard on Preston Mountain. The ninety-seven acres, shaped in a triangle, lay out at the southeast corner of the Hoveout Land, just north of Oblong Lott 44. The Mountain's crest there is remarkably level and free of ledge, though huge glacial erratic boulders are common. There is no sign today that anyone ever lived or farmed there. The Appalachian Trail passes through Ambrose's domain.

On April 8, 1775, Ambrose Benson conveyed twenty acres, a part of the "third tract of the Oblong" to Daniel Lake. Ambrose signed with his mark. The deed remained unacknowledged and unrecorded until 1786.[29]

This was only the beginning of disputes over Mountain land. They continue today. But greater conflicts loomed. By 1766, eastern New York exploded in the first of a series of rebellions that would change the structure of society.

Chapter Four
Neighbors and the Tenants' Revolt

IN 1760, PRESTON MOUNTAIN WAS AN ISLAND of near-wilderness surrounded by small, well-established communities. To the east lay Kent in the colony of Connecticut, which New Englanders had settled twenty years before. North of the Mountain, in what is now Amenia, German Palatines named Rau and Winegar had cleared farms. Dover, on the west, had been home to a scattering of Dutch families for thirty years. Quakers from Massachusetts and Rhode Island settled on Quaker Hill and at Webatuck south of Preston Mountain. The Schaghticoke (or Scatacook) Indians had lived on the southeastern flank of the Mountain for unknown generations.

These people were of diverse backgrounds with little in common. Four languages divided them—five, counting the peculiar idiom of the Quakers. Each community centered on a distinct religious faith, which also tended to divide them. To an outsider, these settlements might have seemed like so many foreign countries.

Dover

DOVER WAS NEITHER A VILLAGE NOR A TOWN; it was a neighborhood, a part of Beekman's Patent and Pawlingstown. The name "Dover" appears in two documents of 1721, both of which refer to "Richard Sackett of Dover." Sackett probably named his home area near Wassaic, "Dover." The name survived and eventually attached to the flat lands several miles south of Sackett's farm—"Dover Plains."[1]

Dutchmen from Kingston first settled Dover Plains. By 1729, three men and their families lived in the vicinity: Derrick De Duyster, Jacob Van Campen, and Arie Rosa. The tax lists reveal that De Duyster and

Van Campen were men of means. They both had several children by the time they moved to Dover. De Duyster was an old man by contemporary standards; he was fifty-three in 1729. All three families belonged to the Kingston Dutch Reformed Church.[2]

A map at Adriance Library in Poughkeepsie indicates that De Duyster and Van Campen built homes near the foot of Plymouth Hill. In May 1731, the two men petitioned the justices of the peace of Dutchess County to lay out and build a road from Dover to the landing at the Hudson River in Poughkeepsie.[3]

By 1731 a fourth Dutch family, Jan Oosterhuit and his wife Anaatjen, moved to the valley. Jacob De Witt and Wouter Westerfall followed in 1733 or 1734. Wouter was a favorite of his landlord, Henry Beekman, who wrote of him in 1744: "Wouter Westfall is honest—be favorable to him." The history of Dover says of these families: "These people comprised what could be called the "first wave" of Dover's settlement—six Dutch families, or, based on intermarriage, one Dutch family."[4, 5]

They remained in Dover over the next twenty years. One Martin Van Dueson settled on Wouter Westfall's place during the 1750s. Van Dueson died around 1782, leaving his land in the valley to his sons and grandsons.

These first Dutch settlers were soldiers. They may have settled in Dover at the request or order of the Beekman family to keep order or to resist squatters. In 1737, the Eighth Company of the Dutchess County Militia consisted of fifty-one enlisted men, but only three officers: Jacob Van Campen, captain; Jacob De Witt, lieutenant; and John Oosterhout—all three from Dover.

These Dutch farmers and soldiers lived a long way from their roots. In the 1730s, the nearest Dutch Reformed churches were in Rhinebeck, Red Hook, and Kingston, all a full day's journey on horseback. However, the Dominies (pastors) of these churches baptized the children of the Dover families, but never on a Sunday. The Dominies must have traveled to Dover to baptize the infants on weekdays.

There is no evidence that a Reformed Church existed in Dover until 1775, though it is likely that a congregation had gathered for several years before that. In 1775, Robert Livingston, heir of the Beekmans, deeded or leased (the document is unclear which) to Peter Coen (Kuhn) and Johannes Van Dusen, farmers, fifteen acres in Dover "for the use of a Protestant reformed Dutch church conformable to the Classis of Amsterdam & the Synod of Dortrught for ever. . . ." This land, where the present Valley View Cemetery now stands, was described as a: "tract has been heretofore used & enjoyed by the inhabitants of Dover & appropriated to the use of the publick worship of God & for a burial ground. . . ."[6]

Apparently, other denominations used the meetinghouse built on the Livingston land, along with the reformed Dutch. By 1750, Baptists of English descent were moving into the valley. By then there were primitive industries getting under way along the rivers and streams: an iron forge at Dover Furnace and sawmills and gristmills along the TenMile. Wing Kelley, a Quaker, and Mathias Marsh operated mills along the river.

The English and the Dutch seem to have become good neighbors. Over the next several decades their families intermarried. Some of the Dutch anglicized their names. The descendants of Derick De Duyster changed their surname to "Dutcher." One grandson, Cornelius Dutcher, farmed along the Oblong line at the foot of the mountain in the late 1700s. His next neighbor up on the mountain to the east was Martin Preston.

Amenia

THE OBLONG LOTTS CONTINUED NORTH into the eastern portion of what would later be the town of Amenia. Thomas Wolcott, the father of Preston Mountain resident Luke Wolcott, built a sawmill on the Webatuck Creek in South Amenia. He purchased the mill site in 1760 from Henry Clapp. Thomas was a blacksmith and a farmer in addition to being a miller. His troubles with his father-in-law, John Sackett, were set forth in Chapter Three. Wolcott's place lay between the Sackett family at Wassaic and the Palatine Germans who occupied farms near Amenia Union.

The Palatines were indentured servants that the British Crown brought to America to provide materials for the navy, principally tar. Driven out of the Rhineland by the war with the French, thousands of them became refugees in England. In 1709, the government shipped more than three thousand Palatines to New York. From there they were taken one hundred miles up the Hudson River and encouraged to build camps in the forest at Livingston Manor. Then they set to work distilling tar from the pine trees. They endured a hard lot; bad food, slim provisions, and their own stubbornness all contributed to make a failure of this venture. People who had farmed in the Old World would not settle for this existence. They scattered to find farms in the New World—to Pennsylvania, the Schoharie Valley, and to Dutchess County.

The Raus and the Winegars made their way to the Oblong near the colony line in the 1720s. Uldrick Winegar built a handsome stone house on his farm. The house still stood in 1990. From Amenia Union, Winegar's children and grandchildren moved south through Bog Hollow to Kent. Hendrick Winegar sold a sawmill on Preston Mountain to Abel Rust in 1785. During the Revolution, Hendrick, with his partners, operated the iron forge at Macedonia, north of Kent. His sons continued in the iron business into the nineteenth century. One of them, Garrett, was elected the state representative from Kent.[7]

The Palatines were Lutherans. Like their Dutch neighbors in Dover, they lived far from their church in an age when the church was a part of most peoples' lives.

Kent

BY 1760, KENT, CONNECTICUT, was an ordered and settled New England town. Land in the Housatonic Valley had been divided and redivided among the original proprietors and their offspring until further division was unfruitful. By 1760, young people in Kent were looking for new lands or new occupations.

Iron-making was an obvious choice. There had been a forge in Kent as early as 1744. Wilson's forge at Macedonia and the Converse Forge on Preston Mountain Brook were built in subsequent years. By 1766, an iron forge was in operation at Bull's Bridge. The last three forges were all close enough to Preston Mountain to burn charcoal produced there.[8]

Kent was a Puritan community, dominated by the Congregational Church. Francis Atwater's 1897 History of Kent, Connecticut, says: "The early history of the town is principally that of the Congregational Church, for at that time the town and church were inseparable." From the incorporation of the church in 1738, "a tax of 4d an acre for four years was laid on all divided lands for the support of the ministry. The meetinghouse was completed by 1743, by which time there were nearly seventy members of the church. This was probably the majority of the population of Kent."[9]

Congregational churches, supported by public taxes, were the norm in Connecticut and Massachusetts. Puritanism was effectively a "state religion." The opposite side of that coin was that other faiths were either not tolerated, or barely tolerated, by the Puritan majority.

The Episcopal Church, the Church of England, was barely tolerated. Nominally, the Crown still ruled in colonial Kent, so the Episcopal Church was able to get a start there by 1760, though no building was erected until 1773. By then, the colonists' tolerance for the Church of England was wearing dangerously thin.

> The church was small in numbers; she was hated and despised by the multitude who regarded Episcopacy as hostile to civil as well as religious liberty. When the war [the Revolution] really broke out many of the clergy had to flee, others were persecuted and imprisoned, churches were closed, many of them desecrated and defiled by the mob. [10]

Kent may have been more tolerant than most revolutionary communities. The Episcopal rector Reverend Samuel Clark managed to serve his flock through the entire war. It was not until 1787 that he, along with thousands of Tories, migrated to Nova Scotia. It took twenty years to reorganize an active parish in Kent after the Revolution.

The Society of Friends (Quakers) and the Baptists were faiths that were also barely tolerated by their Puritan neighbors. The opening of the Oblong to settlement sparked decades of migration of Quakers and Baptists to the New York–Connecticut border. Kent, at first, took a dim view of these events. In the 1750s, four members of the Congregational Church were disciplined by their brethren for attending a "disorderly meeting"—a Quaker meeting.[11]

Between 1743 and 1763, Moravian missionaries preached to the Schaghticoke Indians at their village along the Housatonic. The Puritans also disapproved of the Moravians. "Regretfully, the 'brand' of Christianity the Moravians practiced was very different from that of the Connecticut colonists. So different in fact, that Connecticut rejected and opposed the teachings of the Moravian missionaries."[12]

The Moravians succeeded in converting many of the Schaghticokes to Christianity, a fact that probably contributed to the Indians remaining outside the otherwise close-knit fabric of the Kent community.

Kent was always Preston Mountain's closest neighbor, in every sense. Many of the Mountain's settlers came from Kent, including the Prestons. Trading for supplies took place in Kent. Until sawmills were built on the Mountain, timber and grain were milled in Kent. The iron forges, and later the furnaces, consumed charcoal from timber cut and burned on the Mountain. Most of the Mountain's settlers were New Englanders, Yankees who had more in common with their neighbors in Kent than with the other folk around them.[13]

Scatacook or Schaghticoke

THE TRIBE LIVED AT SCATACOOK, on the southeast flank of the Mountain, near the junction of the TenMile and the Housatonic. How long they had been there is unknown. Samuel Orcutt's work, *The Indians of the Housatonic and Naugatuck Valleys*, states:

> That there was a Scatacook tribe or settlement of Indians in what is now Kent before Gideon Mauwehu located there is quite certain, for we find in the Colonial Records, Vol. VI, page 512, the "Scatacook" and "Skatcuk," as designating them a tribe then dwelling there, and of such number and importance as to cause much alarm at the report that they were "all drawn off to the enemy"—the Canada Indians—and therefore twenty-one soldiers were sent to Litchfield, for "scouting, watching and warding for the safety of said town", and fifteen others were sent to New Milford for the same purpose. This was in the spring of the year 1725.[14]

Orcutt goes on to speculate, "it is probable that it [the Scatacook settlement in Kent] had been there many years previous to 1707."[15]

The origin of the Schaghticokes is uncertain. Some historians claimed that they were the refugee remnants of the southern Connecticut Pequots, decimated by the English wars of the seventeenth century. Others believed that the language the Schaghticokes spoke did not derive from the tongue of any New England tribes, but from the New York Indians known as the Mohicans.

Whatever their background, by 1760 the Schaghticokes were a people under stress. Their tribal lands had been deeded away or "leased" by previous sachems and they were left with about two thousand acres between the Housatonic River and the New York border. Though some of this tract was fertile bottomland, most of it was the steep and rocky flanks of Preston Mountain. Though they continued to travel south to the "great falls" at New Milford, their ancestral fishing place, their free and unfettered access to hunting, fishing, and foraging grounds was gone.

The Indians clearly made efforts to adapt to the changing world. They allowed the Moravians to convert them to Christianity, and their warriors served with the colonial militia in two wars.

> Many Schaghticoke men fled the poverty and squalor at home and enlisted in the Connecticut army whenever a war was fought. In the American War of Independence, for instance, nearly all the men of the tribe enlisted on the side of the newborn United States.[16]

The Schaghticokes' efforts to conform to the colonists' ways only made their lives worse. The Yankee clergy misunderstood, or was suspicious of, the Moravian practice of Christianity. Even though many Indians became Christians, their English neighbors failed to recognize their faith. In the wars, so many Indians died that the male population of the tribe was dangerously reduced.[17]

By 1751, the General Assembly of Connecticut resorted to selling the Indians' lands without the consent or the signatures of the native peoples. In 1756, the Schaghticokes petitioned the assembly for the return of a parcel on Preston Mountain that had been sold in this way.

> To the honble General Assembly of the Colony of Connecticutt to be Convaid at New Haven in said Colony on ye 2d Thursday of Octo-r AD 1756 The Prayer and representation of the Chief Sachem and oth-

ers, of the tribe of Indians called the Scatacook Tribe living southwest of the Township of Kent on the West Side of Ousatunuck River – that we have always with Cheerfulness assisted and Joyned the English in all expeditions against King George's Enemies, and have never been Chergeable Burthensome or Troublesome to this Colony by any contentions that some other tribes have occasioned and have always continued in this quiet and peaceful disposition with the English near us by selling our lands for very Trifling Sums...part of those lands, which we are informed have been sold sometime since viz in 1754 by the order of the Assembly...that the half of ye 24th lott sold by the Governments Commss (Commissioners) spreads over a certain Notch in the mountains which is the outlet on walk for us into ye woods. . . ."[18]

The assembly had sold the Schaghticokes' access to their hunting grounds on Preston Mountain, and the Indians wanted it back. They did not get it.

Quaker Hill

QUAKER HILL RISES ACROSS THE VALLEY OF THE TENMILE RIVER, south of Preston Mountain. Topographically it is not unlike the mountain: it rises five hundred to eight hundred feet above the surrounding valleys; it is dotted with higher hills and swamps; and it is a prolific water source. It stretches from south to north about eight miles from Patterson in Putnam County through Pawling into the town of Dover.

Members of the Society of Friends settled Quaker Hill early. Nathan Birdsall and Benjamin Ferris are reputed to have moved there in 1728. Since Nathan Birdsall was one of the surveyors of the original Oblong, it is unlikely that either man moved there before 1731. Nevertheless, there were soon a dozen or more Quaker families on the Hill, among them people named Irish, Wing, Briggs, Toffey, Akin, Taber, Russell, Osborn, Merritt, Dakin, Hoag, and Soule.

Many of the families migrated from Dartmouth, Massachusetts, near New Bedford. Others came from Cape Cod, Nantucket, and Rhode Island. The main attraction was that the hill was in the Oblong so that the land could be purchased, not merely leased. The Quakers thought that they had found a community where they could live and worship and be left alone. They were wrong.

They built a meetinghouse and met there for silent worship. Though they welcomed people of other faiths in their midst, if a Quaker strayed from the flock or "married out of meeting," he or she was "shunned." The meeting (which meant both the congregation as a group and the physical gathering of the people) had broad powers to oversee the personal lives and morals of the flock.

The friends had adopted a manner of speech that set them apart from others. They addressed all people with the familiar "thee" and "thou," instead of "you." The custom sprang from an attempt to level society.[19]

They created prosperous farms; nearly all the men were at least part-time farmers. They worked at other trades as well. In 1755, at least one Quaker worked at various trades, among them laborer, carpenter, weaver, blacksmith, and tailor.

From 1762 on, there was a store on the hill. The Merritt store, run by Daniel and Nehamiah Merritt, was at the corner of roads across from the meetinghouse. Ledgers from the store reflect the accounts of its customers for several years. People who traveled from Pawling in the valley, and from Webatuck to the north, traded there. The only Preston Mountain customer recorded as trading there was John Bolt, who swapped a bushel of flax for his goods.[20]

The Quakers were pacifists. They believed not only that one should not fight, but also that one should not support fighting in any way. Thus, when a Quaker refused to join the militia, his faith also required him to refuse to pay another to fight in his stead. In colonial New York, the law required militia duty for every male over sixteen. Most Quakers refused and were fined for their refusal. In 1757 and 1759, the militia confiscated cows, calves, horses, saddles, teapots, leather breeches, pewter dishes, and sundry other items. George Soule, Nathan Soule's father, lost a cow and a heifer. He and his brethren stood in their yards and watched their neighbors ride off with their goods. There was no appeal.[21]

It was the custom for Quakers who felt so moved to travel from place to place, absorbing the spirit of the various meetings around the colonies, and, sometimes, preaching. John Woolman, from New Jersey, was one such itinerant Quaker. In the spring of 1747, and again in

1760, he visited the Oblong meeting on Quaker Hill. As he had done all over the colonies, he preached against the evils of slavery. In 1767, the Oblong meeting clearly declared its intention of freeing the slaves, one of the first to do so. The movement caught fire throughout the Society of Friends. Within ten years, the last slave owned by a Quaker Hill Friend was freed.[22]

Freeing slaves was not as simple as opening the front door and saying, "go." The Friends initiated the practice (later made law) of insuring that the freed people could support themselves. It was a complicated matter, and it would involve the active participation of the Oblong Quakers for the next forty years. It would also bear fruit on Preston Mountain.

Preston Mountain

THUS SURROUNDED BY PEOPLE OF WIDELY DIFFERENT BACKGROUNDS and values, and by communities already settled into social and religious patterns, the Preston Mountain settlers faced limited choices. Economically, only subsistence farming insured survival. Food, fuel, and shelter came from the land. A surplus or ready cash was required for taxes, staples, weapons, and some tools. Luke Wolcott was a blacksmith. Another man was a tailor, and a third was a cobbler (their identities have not survived). Most residents had no trade. Iron-making was the only available industry, so the Mountain people became colliers, woodcutters, teamsters, and foundrymen.

They made a religious choice. With Baptist, Quaker, Congregational, and Dutch Reformed congregations nearby, and, presumably, available to all, Preston Mountain people joined none of them. In 1805, James Agard's wife, Annah, joined the Kent Congregational Church. She was the first Mountain resident to join a church.[23]

The Tenants' Revolt

THE 1760S WITNESSED THE FIRST MAJOR REBELLION in colonial New York— the Tenants' Revolt. It began in 1766, the year Martin and Rebecca moved to Pawlingstown. Though the rebellion eventually spread to

Westchester County, and even to Manhattan, it began in Pawl-ingstown.

William Prendergast, a farmer in the town, led the revolt. His wife, born Mehitabel Wing, was the daughter of Quakers from the Oblong Meeting. Prendergast and his neighbors rebelled against an entrenched plutocracy and a system of land ownership and feudal tenure that had disappeared in most of the world. Farmers in Pawl-ingstown did not own their land; they were tenants of the Beekman family or the Phillipse family, to whom they paid a rent. The payments sometimes took the form of cash money, but, more often, it was grain or fowl or a "day's riding"—work for the landlord. Their tenure was limited. A farmer could not pass on a lifetime's work in husbandry and improvements on the land to his sons; nor could he convey his farm to another for value. He could work the land, and live on it, or he could walk away. If he had a bad year and could not pay the rent, the landlord could take back the farm and seize his goods (livestock and equipment) in payment for the rent. In addition, the tenant could grind his grain only at the landlord's mill, and he was required to offer his grain for sale to the landlord first.

Those farmers who failed to meet the lease requirements were evicted. If they tried to defend themselves, they found that the landlords had retained the only lawyers in the colony. A wave of bitterness over these conditions grew through the years and finally broke in the spring of 1766. Staughton Lynd described what happened next:[25]

> During the winter, in the after-harvest talk at Morrison's and Towner's taverns, a plan of action had crystallized and was now put into effect. When May came no rents were paid. Tenants who attempted to make an individual settlement were visited at night by groups of their neighbors armed with clubs and rifles. William Prendergast, a well-respected man rather more prosperous than most of his following, was induced to become the tenants' leader. A committee of twelve was set up to assist him, militia companies were formed and captains elected. Local justices of the peace were forbidden to serve judicial process on days when the tenants were meeting; the tenants undertook to rescue any of their number who should be imprisoned.[25]

These rebel militias paraded up and down the countryside and made a show of force that probably shocked their fellow colonists. Agrarian uprisings would one day be an American pastime, but the first one was unique. Colonists were used to a stable society in which everyone knew his or her place and remained there. The landlord class controlled that society. The Dutchess County sheriff was James Livingston, of the powerful clan of Livingston Manor. The web of landlord dominance spread over the entire government of the colony.

> [O]f the one hundred and thirty-seven persons who held any of the executive, legislative and judicial offices indicated above from about the middle of the century to the Revolution, one hundred and ten, or eighty percent, were large landowners, or related to such families. . . . Against such an array of landlord power, what prospect of improving his lot did the small farmer have in an appeal to executive, legislative or judicial remedies?[26]

Until 1766, control of society had been maintained peacefully. This time things would be different.

Armed mobs visited the homes where men had been ejected, dispossessed the new tenants Robinson had put in (Beverly Robinson, a large landholder of Southern Dutchess County), and restored the original occupants. When one of their comrades, John Way, was imprisoned in Poughkeepsie, the tenants turned up in force, overawed the sheriff and justices, and took Way home with them. This was on June 6, 1766. The next men the authorities captured were jailed in New York City. The tenants then marched on the city, confidently expecting welcome and assistance from the metropolitan Sons of Liberty. When this failed to materialize, they hesitated on the outskirts of the city and finally went back home.[27]

The landlords knew that Prendergast was teaching the poor something new. Every day that his rebellion lasted, more tenants, laborers, and mechanics awakened to the notion that the established order might be changed. At least two thousand tenant farmers had joined his ranks. Prendergast had to be stopped.

Sheriff Livingston could not depend on the loyalty of the local militia. Sloops loaded with cardinal-coated British soldiers sailed up the Hudson, and the troops debarked at Poughkeepsie. They marched on Quaker Hill. When the soldiers reached the homes of rebellious tenants, they "burnt and destroyed some of their houses, pillaged and plundered others, stove in their cider barrels, turned their provisions…out into the open streets, ripped open their feather beds."[28] There were skirmishes with the rebels, but no pitched battles. One British soldier was killed.

A defiant William Prendergast awaited the troops on Quaker Hill. "Armed with a cutlass, he vowed that he was determined to 'make day light shew thro' anyone who opposed him." But Prendergast was overwhelmed and carried off in irons to jail. The revolt subsided while the tenants waited for his trial, which took place at the July assizes in Poughkeepsie. The judges, "the greatest landlords and land speculators of the colony," [29] traveled to Poughkeepsie to hear the case. Among them was William Smith, co-owner of tracts 3 and 4 of the Oblong on Preston Mountain. High treason was charged against Prendergast. Unlike his sixty codefendants, who all pled guilty to lesser offenses and were pilloried for their crimes, he faced execution.

The trial lasted twenty-four hours. Mehitabel Prendergast was her husband's only lawyer. She made a profound impression on everyone; so much so that the prosecutor moved to remove her from the court, "lest she might too much influence the jury by her very Looks." The court overruled him, and Mehitabel argued on.[30]

The judges found Prendergast guilty. His wife promptly mounted a horse and rode off to New York to seek a reprieve. Meanwhile the court sentenced William:

> that the prisoner be led back to the Place where he came and from shall be drawn on a hurdle to the place for execution, and then shall be hanged by the neck, and then shall be cut down alive, and his Entrails and Privy members shall be cut from his Body, and shall be burned in his Sight, and his Head shall be cut off, and his Body shall be divided into four parts and shall be disposed of at the King's Pleasure.[31]

Those settlers who could read learned of this gruesome sentence in the *Gazette* or the *Mercury* in the late summer of 1766. Others heard of it from talk in the taverns. Meanwhile, the king's troops continued to burn and pillage the homes of the rebels, planting the seeds of 1776.

The execution date was set for September 26, 1766. The sheriff advertised for an executioner, promising that he "will meet with a good reward, [and] he shall be disguised so as not to be known, and secured from insults." Sheriff Livingston attracted no takers. Faced with an angry and sullen citizenry, Governor Moore granted a reprieve to Prendergast on September 1, 1766. The next day, fifty farmers attempted to spring him from the jail in Poughkeepsie, but he declined to escape. Eventually, he was released.[32]

The damage was done. The revolt bore a harvest. The poor farmers of Dutchess County learned to despise the king's government and the rich landholders it represented. The land claims of men like William Smith might be contested by adverse possession or by force if necessary. The 1766 revolt also fostered a spirit of lawlessness that would take root and grow into a form of guerilla warfare during the Revolution ten years later. For the moment, the lawbreakers confined themselves to stealing horses and counterfeiting notes, activities for which the Dover area was notorious. In 1768, the citizens of Dover sought protection from outlaws by presenting a petition to the Court of General Sessions, claiming, "we have not a constable within ten miles." Martin Preston signed the petition.[33]

No Preston Mountain resident's name appears on the rolls of those who participated in the Tenants' Revolt. They were not tenants—they paid rent to no man, and they considered themselves freeholders. Martin Preston must have known how fragile his land claim was and that his competitor was the powerful lawyer William Smith. For the next few years, Martin kept a low profile and held onto his land.

Chapter Five
"The Poor and Distressed"

THE TURMOIL OF 1766 coincided with the settling of Preston Mountain. Over the next twenty years, most of the land on the Mountain that could be farmed at all was cleared, and some of it was fenced. By the end of the Revolution, Martin and Rebecca Preston had neighbors named Agard, Philleo, Cummins, Bradshaw, Mathews, Bolt, Rust, Kennedy, Wolcott, Wheeler, Roberts, and others. Within a generation, they would be related by marriage to many of these families. The Preston Mountain community had begun.

On February 12, 1772, Martin Preston and two other men attempted to perfect their titles to three parcels of four hundred acres each on Preston Mountain. Ebenezer Judd (Rebecca's nephew) and Aaron Pain, both of Kent, joined Martin in his petition to Governor Tyron of New York. They asked for a total of twelve hundred acres of the Hoveout Lands. They claimed to be "poor inhabitants" who had, for several years, settled and improved parts of the Mountain, and,

> Not only paid a valuable consideration therefor but have expended their little subsistence, and their whole labor and industry for years in endeavouring (illegible) support for themselves and their families from that rough and mountainous tract of land.[1]

The petition went on to say that they believed they had acquired title, but,

> that the persons from whom they purchased had no manner of Title to the said Mountain but occupancy and that the same remains unpatented and vested in the Crown, and the persons from whom

they purchased having absconded and being very poor your petitioners have no recourse but your Excellency's well known [illegible] and his tenderness toward the poor and distressed.[2]

In their petition, Martin and his partners clearly recognized William Smith's and James Brown's patent for the six hundred acre "Fourth Tract of the Oblong." The petition purported to exclude the fourth tract from the land prayed for. But the petitioners did not clearly describe the land they sought. Martin Preston failed to advise Governor Tyron that Martin's farmstead was located square in the middle of Smith's and Brown's fourth tract.

The year 1772 must have been a prime year for attempts at bamboozling Governor Tyron. In July, a Dover man, Jeremiah French, and one Henry Conroy, petitioned the governor for the same land that Martin and friends had sought earlier in the year. French and Conroy based their request on the perceived need for the Church of England in the Dover area. To support and church and its clergy, they said a glebe would be necessary. A glebe was a parcel of land intended to provide income for a church. French and Conroy thought that the two thousand acres of Hoveout Lands on Preston Mountain would suffice for this purpose.[3]

The governor granted neither petition. Perhaps Tyron had learned that both petitions failed to state important facts. Martin Preston and his compatriots had already settled on lands that the prestigious Crown subject William Smith claimed. Jeremiah French sought land that had already been settled by others.

Probably, if Tyron could have divined into the future, he would have granted the French/Conroy petition. Within five years, Jeremiah French would be a notorious Dover Tory. Within five years, Preston Mountain would be a hotbed of Patriot militia. If the Mountain Patriots learned of French's designs, it must have spurred their anger at all things English.

Now, a new generation of settlers braved the uncertainties of Hoveout titles to claim land on the Mountain. It is possible to guess at the locations of their old farms by examining a topographical map of the area. The farmers needed little—a few acres of near-level ground close to a water source and reachable by some manner of road.

Abel Rust arrived after the Revolution. His place lay just inside New York on the road from Macedonia, a few hundred yards northwest of Duck Pond. Abel's father was Simeon Rust, who, in 1771, received a grant of two hundred seventy-three acres in Kent from the colony of Connecticut. Simeon was a rugged man. His descendants said of him, "he was very smart up to the day he died; in the morning he hopped on his horse, rode off at a canter and before night he was dead."[4]

His son, Abel, was also a vigorous man. He lived to age ninety-five. At eighteen, he married Lesen Sprague in Kent. In 1785, he purchased a sawmill from Hendrick Winegar. The mill was located at the state line on Bolt Brook (Preston Mountain Brook), "south of the rattlesnake den." Abel's home was nearby. Many years later he conveyed the mill and the farm to an elderly Martin Preston and his youngest son, John Preston II.[5]

The Rust place was a true mountain farm. There were a few acres of level land near the house, but the mountain rose steeply from there to the top of "Rust Mountain," north of the buildings. The best land lay on top of the mountain. Here, Abel cleared and walled fifteen or twenty acres of meadow and plow land. Abel joined the army early in the Revolution and served with distinction.

His next neighbor to the west was probably Luke Wolcott, who was also a soldier. This farm was at the southeast corner of Wolf Swamp. During the nineteenth century, the farm belonged to Luke Wolcott's descendants, but there is no recorded deed to Luke. The foundation for the large house remains on a small knob surrounded by stone walls. This farm was broken up into scattered parcels of tillage and pasture bounded by swamp. Walled clearings still exist north of Wolf Swamp, a long way from the Wolcott house, but obviously once part of the farm. Luke Wolcott's son Thomas married Martin and Rebecca Preston's daughter Abigail.[6]

Further west, along the east side of the Kennedy Bridge Brook (now Crane Pond), Hugh Kennedy and his son Gideon cleared a small farm. Gideon married Elizabeth Preston. The walled fields slope south from the road. The cellar hole of their home rests in a hollow west of a small swamp. The Kennedys laid out their orchard on the north slope of a nearby hill. The pioneers had learned the value of planting orchards on the north slopes. This retarded development of fruit blossoms and saved the trees from frost damage. Apples commanded a central role on eighteenth century farms. In addition to being eaten fresh, dried, sauced, or baked, they were the chief ingredients in the pioneers' favorite beverage—cider. An orchard was a comfort to the farmer.

East of the Kennedy place, and just east of the modern road to Depression Pond, Valentine Wheeler laid out a homestead. The house sat in a north-sloping glen beneath the high mountain to the east. A walled close surrounded the house and a spring rose from the ground nearby. There were small fields on the hillsides around the house.

Valentine may never have lived on this farm since he also owned a farm down the valley in Dover. When he died in 1782, his will referred to the Mountain farm:

> I leave to my son John the farm where Adam Coon now lives, running south as far as my land goes to John Bolt's land, and then in a straight line to the top of the bald mountain, from thence to the French Doctor's [Benjamin Delavergne] former line.[7]

The "bald mountain" was the peak now shown as 1,414 feet high on the topographic map. It remains nearly bald today.

John Bolt's farm (or the farmstead itself) now lies submerged beneath Depression Pond. There is little known about John Bolt. He had a son, John Jr., and a daughter, Huldah. She married Abijah Patchin, and their family remained on the Mountain for a hundred years. Bolt Brook, named for the family, begins at Depression Pond.

Abel Rust, Luke Wolcott, Hugh, and Gideon Kennedy, Valentine Wheeler and John Bolt all pioneered small subsistence farms—homesteads too small or too rough to produce a surplus. Swamps, ledges, and boulders encroached on their holdings. Down in the valleys, their neighbors and relatives could gradually enlarge and improve their farms until wealth replaced subsistence. The early settlers on Preston Mountain had no such opportunity. Still, in the beginning, the Mountain rewarded the farmers with unique soil conditions. Ages of deep shade beneath first growth timber left a thick layer of rotted leaves and vegetation—primeval humus. Unlike the valley bottomland, there was no sod to be broken. The Mountain farm could produce good crops with relatively little labor compared to the valley farms, at least at first. But the mountain farms produced abundant crops of stones too; each winter's frost heaved up another batch to be carted off on a stone boat, or lugged away by hand.

At first, the settlers must have been pleased with the fertility of their land. The thin black soil was naturally fertile. Despite the stumps and stones, the ground was easy to work. But it was rarely level, and it eroded easily in the spring freshets and snowmelt. Erosion accelerated as the forests were cut. Iron-making magnified the problem because the demand for charcoal, plus the household need for fuel, required huge amounts of wood. An ordinary dwelling needed twenty cords of wood a year for fuel. It would not be long before the hills on Preston Mountain would be bare of trees. When the trees were gone the soil disappeared with them.

By leveling the forests, the settlers removed another asset from their balance sheets—chestnuts. Scientists today estimate that one in four trees in eighteenth century eastern forests was an American chestnut. These trees produced huge crops of nuts. Chestnuts were said to have covered the ground like marbles. Animals and people browsed the woods for chestnuts, and the nuts were a staple in the diets of hogs. They roamed the woods, unrung and unfenced, fattening on acorns, hickory nuts, and chestnuts. The farmers carved out designs in their pigs' ears—earmarks—to distinguish their animals from those of their neighbors. In most of the area, the practice of earmarking died out around the beginning of the nineteenth century because free-roaming hogs were dangerous to people and destructive to property. But the Preston Mountain farmers continued to earmark animals until well into the nineteenth century. The marks were recorded in local records. Most communities required that hogs be rung (carry rings in their snouts so they couldn't root), but on the frontier they went without them, presenting hazards to other beasts and to children.[8]

The woodcutting, charcoal-making, and wall-building meant that huge volumes of timber, charcoal, and stone had to be moved. Oxen did the hauling. The creaking of the carts and yokes, and the lowing of the beasts must have been constantly in the settlers' hearing. A farmer across the Hudson River in Orange County, New York, Hector St. John de Crevecoeur, described the use of oxen on a hill farm:

> In the rough, stony parts of New England, they use no other team but oxen; and no people on earth understand the management of them better. They shoe them with admirable skill and neatness. They are coupled with a yoke which plays loose on their necks. It is fastened with a bow which is easily taken off or put on. They draw by the tops of their shoulders.
>
> Besides a wagon, most farmers have an ox cart, which is fitted to carry heavy stones and large timbers. With these we convey logs to the sawmills by suspending them under the axle-tree of the cart. A good one, well shod with iron, costs twenty dollars.[9]

When the working life of an ox came to end it became beef for the family.

The settlers needed other animals as well: a cow, a horse, a hog or two, and the occasional sheep. The women milked the cow for milk, butter, and cheese. For those who could afford it, the horse provided transportation. Most folks traveled as a part of their work, hauling something. But the need for horses increased as the Revolution approached.

To ensure a continuous supply of young stock, someone in the neighborhood kept a stallion, a bull, a boar, and other males of various species. These beasts were difficult and dangerous. They required stout barns and fences, and a stouthearted farmer to manage them. Perhaps Martin Preston had lived there long enough to own a barn and fencing strong enough to contain such animals. Managing the breeding process was a community project. The owner of the female animal observed her carefully for weeks, and led her to the farm of the owner of the male of the species when she came into estrus. Then the two farmers worked to bring the animals together without injury either to the animals or themselves. It was essential and dangerous work. Bulls and stallions gored and kicked without reason or warning. Injuries and deaths were common.

A custom of cooperation grew. Neighbors helped each other clear land, stone fields, build walls, and harvest crops—any labor-intensive task called for teamwork. The farmers traded their time and their strength. Men and boys moved from farm to farm, working through each season's jobs. Women followed with food. Such communal work provided opportunity for fun and social gatherings. When the children husked corn or the men raised a barn, the gathering became a "frolic."

> The name "frolic" may perhaps scandalize you and make you imagine that we meet to riot together. Lest you should misunderstand me, give me leave to explain myself. I really know among of us no custom which is so useful and tends so much to establish the union and the little society which subsists among us. Poor as we are, if we have not the gorgeous balls, the harmonious concerts, the shrill horn of Europe, yet we dilate our hearts as well with the simple Negro fiddle, and with our rum and water, as you do with your delicious wines. In the summer, it often happens that either through sickness or accident, some families are not able to do all they must do. Are we afraid, for instance, that we shall not be able to break up our summer fallow? In due time we invite a dozen neighbors, who will come with their teams and finish it all in one day. At dinner with give them the best victuals our farm affords; there are feasts the goodness of which greatly depends on the knowledge and ability of our wives. Pies; puddings; fowls roasted and boiled – nothing is spared that can evince our gratitude. In the evening, the same case is repeated, after which young girls and lads generally come from all parts to unite themselves to the assembly. As they have done no work, they generally come after the supper and partake of the general dance. I have never been so happy in my life as when I have assisted at these simple merriments, and indeed they are the only ones I know. Each returns home happy and is satisfied, and our work is done.[10]

The pioneer placed a priority on barns. The barn housed the animals and their feed and the most crucial workspace on the farm—the threshing floor. Placed between the haymows, with large doors on either side, the threshing floor was the surface on which wheat oats and rye were flailed to separate the grain. The doors were opened, the wind blew across the floor, and the farmer and his family tossed scoops of grain into the air to "winnow," or separate kernel from chaff. Here, too, they husked corn and cleaned flax. With a dry haymow above and a warm stable below, the barn gave the family security.

Most of the early homes on Preston Mountain were rude huts—log cabins or board cottages. Of the cellar holes remaining on the Mountain, only those of Martin Preston, Luke Wolcott, and Abel Rust seem to have borne homes of any size. Later, settlers built substantial homes, two of which remain at the north end of East Mountain Road. But the standard was a dirt-floored cabin.

Enoch Philleo built such a cabin (his surname was also spelled "Fillow"). Enoch and his parents and his brothers, Samuel and Phineas, moved to Pawlingstown from Norwalk, Connecticut, in the 1750s. A sister, Esther, was born here in 1757. A descendant described Enoch's place on Preston Mountain: "I can hardly describe the poverty and baldness of the life I saw at his house, a rude log hut, earthen floor, a life entirely barren of refinement."[11]

The Fillow family genealogy described his farm as follows:

> The homestead is only marked by a few old apple trees and a foundation stone. It was situated on Flat Rocks near a cold spring on the old road from E. Mountain to Kent, Ct., one-half mile from any civilization now. He had a large peach orchard and grapes in abundance. It is now (1882) called by the owner "the Enoch Place."[12]

The exact location of Enoch Philleo's cabin is unknown. Because it was on the old road to Kent and on property belonging to Mrs. Clark Preston in 1882, the home was probably located on the hill just east of the last house on East Mountain Road. The old walled road, overgrown now with trees, crosses that spot before turning northeast toward Kent.

Enoch was a lively man, something of a character. He participated in every event, except, apparently, caring for his own family. He served as a minuteman during the Revolution, leaving his young wife, Sarah, sister of James Agard, to fend for herself. Together they had ten children, several of whom lived extraordinary lives despite their impoverished childhoods.

James Agard married Annah Judd, Rebecca Preston's sister, and they built their house on the east side of East Mountain Road on the bend just north of the hill marked 1,231 feet on the topographical map.

They had five daughters, four of whom married sons of Preston Mountain residents. One of them was Peter Roberts who married Diadema Agard. Peter's father, Daniel, owned a place just west of the Agards on the crest of the hill overlooking the TenMile River.[13]

The Harrington place was along the Connecticut border just north of Preston Hill. The Harringtons lived elsewhere. Their tenants were Enoch Philleo's sister Esther and her husband, William Bradshaw. William was unique among his neighbors; living among so many Patriots, William was a Tory. Though he never owned his home, it was always known thereafter as "William Bradshaw lands."[14]

There were others who moved onto the Mountain in the 1770s and 1780s. The tax lists reflected a large population by the end of the Revolution. Where they all lived is a mystery. The dirt-floor cabins or huts of the some of the pioneers left no trace or ruin. The homesteads of Joseph Agard, Phineas Philleo, Samuel Philleo, Charles Blowers, Patrick Kidney, Justus Mathews, Silas Ray, and Benjamin Owens lie somewhere on the Mountain. All these men's names, along with others whose homes can now be located, appear in the 1790 federal census. Many of them were gone by the 1800 census.

While new neighbors filled the land around them, Martin and Rebecca Preston improved their home and farm. Grief also entered their lives. Sometime before 1774, Rebecca bore two more sons, Martin Jr. and Aaron. Both boys died young, perhaps at birth. They were probably buried in the cemetery on the hill south of their parent's home, but no monument to them survives.[15]

Then, in 1774, Rebecca gave birth to twins, Philip and Abigail; both twins survived to marry and bring their own children into the world. By 1774, their son Timothy was thirteen and able to help with the farm work. Their other sons David and Obadiah were striplings, helpers and nuisances by turns.

Martin cleared land continuously, felling trees and stoning fields. The useful area around the farmstead increased each year. While his new neighbors struggled to subdue enough land to feed their families, Martin worked toward a surplus. The hills around his home still bear witness to his labor—acres of pasture and plow land, much of it fenced.

But, his life was not all work; he found time to hunt and to develop his reputation as a mighty hunter. He also indulged his hobby of beekeeping. Honey was not a luxury. Apart from maple sugar, the frontiersman had no other sugar for his palate. Honey sweetened his tea and his children's corn meal mush. It also made a liquor that was a substitute for cider.

Obtaining honey was an art. He could not send for mail-order bees. If he wanted honey he had to find the bees himself. If he wanted a continuous supply of honey, he had to bring the bees home. In the spring, when the seed was in the ground, Martin took off a few days and spent them in the woods. He took a gun, a blanket, food, wax, vermilion, honey, and a small pocket compass. Hector St. John de Crevecoeur described the pioneer bee hunt:

> With these implements, I proceed to such woods as are at a considerable distance from any settlements. I carefully examine whether they abound with large trees; if so, I make a small fire on some flat stones in a convenient place; on the fire I put some wax; close by the fire, on another stone, I drop honey in distinct drops, Which I surround with small quantities of vermilion, laid on the stone; and then I retire carefully to watch whether any bees appear.[16]

If the bees did appear, and they often did, they would fly home with the vermilion on their bodies. Martin would observe their course with his compass. He would guess at the time it took for them to return. By following his compass and estimating the distance of the bees' flight, he found the tree where they swarmed. He was then in a position to bring them home.

Martin made some of the honey into the ancient English drink called mead. He cut the sweetness with apple brandy, which converted the beverage into metheglin. Martin's metheglin had a following.[17]

In future years, the Prestons would contribute the land for a public cemetery on the Mountain, and, later, a schoolhouse. They were there to stay. Unlike their neighbors, they remained absorbed in their own business. Before long, Timothy, David, and Obadiah married, and, for a while, farmed their own places on the Mountain. When the Revolution came along and tore apart the foundations of colonial society, the Prestons stayed home.

Chapter Six
"The Revolution:
To Suppress the Internal Foes"

THE STANDARD HISTORIES of the American Revolution tell the stories of the major battles: the siege of Boston, Long Island, Saratoga, Monmouth, and Yorktown. The treachery of Arnold and the cool courage of Nathan Hale provide sidelights to the main drama.

For the common people of the American colonies, the Revolution meant eight years of bitter feuds between neighbors. The rebel colonists established "Committees of Safety" and charged them with the responsibility of determining the loyalties of their fellow citizens. Minutemen dragged people from their beds. Bands of Tories burned barns and stole horses. Neighbors informed on neighbors. Suspicion and distrust permeated daily life.

Some places were relatively peaceful; these were areas where the population was mostly Rebel or mostly Tory. Where the farmers and villagers were of one accord there was no conflict. Dutchess County, with partisans on both sides, knew no peace.

The County Committee also adopted a pledge, an oath of loyalty to the Rebel cause; every male between the ages of sixteen and sixty was required to sign. In May 1775, the Provincial Congress produced a similar pledge and formed Committees of Safety in each town with instructions to obtain signatures on the oath and to assure compliance with it. More than a third of Dutchess County men refused to sign the oath. The records for Pawlingstown burned, thus obscuring the allegiances of its citizens.[1]

Those who signed the pledge agreed, "that we will in all Things follow the advice of our general Committee respecting the Purposes aforesaid, the Preservation of Peace and good order, and the Safety of Individuals and private Property." The colonists thus placed their liberties in the hands of their neighbors, many of whom maintained a lively and unhealthy interest in the affairs of others.[2]

Most men sided with one cause or the other. Both sides mistreated those who remained neutral (like the Quakers). Choosing sides was a vital decision. Picking the losing side risked the loss of land, home, and possessions, and, sometimes, life itself. Nevertheless, thousands of colonists made the choice openly so that all could know whether they were Tory or Whig (Rebel). At the same time, many of them began to think of themselves not as "colonists" or "Englishmen," but as Americans. The poor and landless were now freeholders; the rebellion seemed intoxicating.

The first Preston Mountain citizen to enlist (though he lived in Kent at the time) was Abel Rust, the sawmiller. He signed on with Colonel Hinman's Regiment of the Connecticut Line. He was eighteen years old. The "line" was not a militia unit; it was the regular army. Unlike the militia, its commander could move the line outside Connecticut.[3]

Typically, the enlistment process offered the opportunity for a frolic. Young men and boys gathered in a public place, often near a tavern where they encountered the recruiters with their drum. Rum and cider flowed. Someone challenged the men by placing a dollar piece on the drumhead. Watched by his peers, the eager recruit took up the dollar and signed his name or made his mark on the enlistment roll. Not to be outdone, others followed. The recruiters ordered their new charges to equip themselves and return ready for duty.

As soon as Abel Rust returned, he marched north with his regiment, through Massachusetts and into the "Hampshire Grants." There they added to the small army of Ethan Allen's Green Mountain Boys and other Connecticut troops commanded by Benedict Arnold. In the early morning hours of May 10, 1775, they rowed across Lake Champlain and captured Fort Ticonderoga.

Sergeant Abel Rust

WHEN THE YOUNG RUST MARCHED OFF THAT SPRING, he faced a life unlike anything in his experience. Though he was probably tough and strong from working in the woods and fields, he would no longer have access to a healthy diet or a warm bed. In theory, Congress supplied provisions for the soldiers. In practice the soldiers shifted for themselves. They often starved. A typical ration was sea bread stored in casks. Someone knocked the head off a barrel; each man grabbed as much of the biscuit as he could when he marched past. One man wrote, "the bread was hard enough to break the teeth of a rat."[4]

With salt fish and scorched Indian corn, the sea bread was supposed to keep life's flames burning. Often, the army could supply none of these victuals. The soldiers formed foraging parties to beg or steal anything edible. These forays tested the loyalties of farmers near the army. Those who cooperated cheerfully were left with a surplus; those who resisted or complained were plucked clean.

The troops slept where they could. Barns and haystacks provided choice accommodations. More often, the men lay on the ground in all weather. Their clothing was homemade, blankets were rare, and boots fell apart. They slept cradling their muskets with the firelocks between their thighs to keep the weapons dry. They had to "weather it out."[5]

Disease was the most dangerous enemy and smallpox the worst of it. The army initiated a program of inoculation against smallpox in field hospitals set up for that purpose. One such hospital was in the Hudson Highlands where Abel Rust received his inoculation. Soldiers there contracted a mild form of the disease (usually) within two or three days of inoculation. Pustules the size of peas formed at the site, leaving a scar when the pus drained from them. Those who survived the treatment usually went back to their units within two or three weeks. But it could be a difficult experience. As a result of his inoculation, Abel Rust wore a lock of snow-white hair for the rest of his life, perhaps from the shock of the treatment.[6]

Abel served seven months for his first enlistment; he was discharged on December 1, 1775. That same day he reenlisted for another year and began a march to Boston. Short enlistments characterized the American army. Most of the soldiers were farmers. If they were not at home to put in the crops, or to harvest them, they feared their families or their animals might starve. The short enlistments presented Washington with a grave problem early in the war. But many loyal soldiers, like Abel Rust, returned to their duty again and again.

In December 1775, Washington faced his first enlistment crisis. The Americans laid siege to the British in Boston, but their army was about to dissolve.

> On December 10, the enlistments of all Connecticut and Rhode Island troops would terminate, and the service-weary men who had been six months from home would be free to return to their hearth sides. Unless, before the end of the year, the General could persuade most of the men to re-enlist, his seige [sic] lines would be empty and overnight his dream of victory would vanish.[7]

The rolls of the army filled up through the winter of 1775–1776. Washington drew the noose tighter around Boston. In March, the British evacuated the city and sailed off to the south. On April 4, 1776, Rust and the rest of the American army started the long overland march to New York. Their route took them across the Housatonic River at Bulls' Falls in Kent, through the Oblong, just south of Preston Mountain, and into Pawlingstown (now Dover). They camped for the night on the plains just west of Wingdale. Washington stayed in a house within sight of his troops.[8]

Probably, most citizens made a point of seeing the Patriot army as it passed. Most countrymen had never seen hundreds of men together, let alone thousands. Perhaps word of the army's movements reached the Oblong by newspaper or word of mouth. The sight of the actual soldiers, en masse, the same troops who had successfully besieged Boston, must have given spirit to the Patriot sympathizers.

During that summer, more Preston Mountain men joined the rebellion. On August 3, Justice (or Justus) Mathews enrolled in Captain Pearce's Company of Minute Men. At forty years of age, Justice was an old man by contemporary standards. The rolls describe him as 5'6" tall with a brown complexion, black hair and eyes—occupation: "taylor." He left a wife, Irena, and their homestead on the Mountain.[9]

Several men signed on with the Company of Minute Men commanded by Captain Cornelius Van Wyck. Enoch Filleo (Philleo) left home to enlist on July 30, 1776. Though his age was recorded as seventeen, he was probably twenty-two or twenty-three. The rolls show him as a farmer, 5'6 1/2" tall with a "fresh complexion," brown eyes, and light hair. Enoch left a sweetheart behind, seventeen-year-old Sarah Agard. Sixty years later she would remember that when Enoch enlisted, he "borrowed or took a gun belonging to her brother, James Agard, as it was a favorite gun of his [James']." James Agard and his wife Annah lived nearby with their daughters.[10]

Enoch went away for a full year. He came home briefly in the autumn of 1777 to attend the funeral of his brother Elijah. Then he was off again until the following spring. Enoch and Sarah were married in April 1780 in New Milford. She sewed a special coat for her husband, the kind worn by minutemen, with fringe decorating the bottom and the neck.

Sarah became pregnant with her first child, a son who would be named Martin. Enoch left again. The new bride suffered. By her own testimony:

> While she was sick and confined with her first child and she was in consequence of the absence of the said Enoch Philleo and her sickness removed to her father (Joseph Agard) where she remained until he the said Enoch Philleo returned which was the summer of 1781 (do not recall the month). . . .[11]

The family genealogy says that the baby, Martin Philleo, was named for Martin Luther. It's possible he was named for their neighbor, Martin Preston; their next child was named Abel. Their third son, Darius, grew up to marry Abel Rust's daughter, Lury. Sarah bore Enoch nine sons in the years they lived on Preston Mountain. The only daughter, Lucinda, died in infancy.[12]

Enoch's older brother Phineas, age twenty-six, enlisted with his brother. He was a tall man, five feet, eleven inches. His wife, Silence, was the sister of Simeon Cummins, who lived down the road a half-mile from Martin and Rebecca Preston at "Schoolhouse Corners."[13]

Phineas and Enoch's future brother-in-law, William Bradshaw, joined up the same day. The rolls describe him as a twenty-year-old farmer, five feet, seven and a half inches tall with a pale complexion, gray eyes, and black hair. The spirit that moved him to join the Rebel cause later abandoned him; he became an active Loyalist.[14]

Roswell Dart (or Darte), the old French and Indian War veteran, enlisted the day before his fellows. There is no evidence that Dart ever lived on the Mountain. However, in 1786 he signed a petition claiming he had settled there. Roswell was a carpenter, thirty-six years old. These minutemen would soon see action. [15]

Two Preston Mountain men were elected officers in the 3rd Regiment of Dutchess County Militia. Luke Wolcott became a second lieutenant on October 17, 1775. He was twenty years old. His son Thomas was a one-year-old toddler. Thomas would grow up to marry Martin and Rebecca Preston's daughter Abigail. On the same October day, Valentine Wheeler was commissioned afirst lieutenant in the same regiment. He was thirty-four years old.[16]

Their commander was Captain Peter Coons. His grave at Valley View Cemetery in Dover Plains reads: "Capt. Peter Kuhn, who died September (?), 1795." He was buried next to Valentine Wheeler's parents, Ephraim Wheeler and Anna Catherina Kuhn Wheeler. Valentine's grave is nearby. The surname "Kuhn" was anglicized into "Coons." Peter Coons was probably Valentine Wheeler's first cousin.

Wheeler served part-time in the militia. He remained at home in Pawlingstown from 1778 to 1781, sufficient time to serve the town as assessor and overseer of the poor. He held some office each year. Peter

White Plains and the Danbury Raid

After a succession of defeats in August and September, Washington abandoned Manhattan and moved his army north into Westchester County. At the end of October, the British attacked the Americans on the hills at White Plains, where the Americans whipped them. On October 31, near White Plains, Captain Van Wyck's minutemen encountered the enemy.

> He [Captain Van Wyck]. . .went out in the morning with about 30 men; fell in with about 100 of the enemy in a house not far distant from their lines; charged them with spirit; gave them a brisk fire; but unfortunately when loading his piece the second time was shot in the head and fell dead; his lieutenant shot down the man who killed his captain. The enemy fled; our party brought off their captain, and yesterday evening I had him interred with the honours of war. He was a good man and a valiant officer.[17]

There were only fifty-two men carried on the rolls of Captain Van Wyck's Company. If thirty of them accompanied their captain that day, some of the Preston Mountain men probably fought in the fatal skirmish.

By 1777, the war moved south to New Jersey and Pennsylvania. Soldiers of the "line," like Abel Rust, marched south with their commander. The militia and the minutemen remained in New York. They did not necessarily go home, but manned any of the several garrisons along the Hudson or in the Highlands. That spring, British troops raided nearby Danbury, Connecticut. They intended to destroy equipment and provisions stored there for the Continental Army. The king's soldiers carried out their mission with a ferocity that the Americans would remember.

> We staid but a short time here [at Newtown, Connecticut], but went on to Danbury, where I had an ample opportunity to see the devastation caused there by the British. The town

had been laid in ashes, a number of the inhabitants murdered and cast into their burning homes, because they presumed to defend their persons and property, or to be avenged on a cruel, vindictive invading enemy. I saw the inhabitants, after the fire was out, endeavouring to find the burnt bones of their relatives amongst the rubbish of their demolished houses. The streets, in many places, were literally flooded by the fat which ran from the piles of barrels of pork burnt by the enemy. –They fully executed their design.[18]

Coons was overseer of the poor in 1778. It seems significant that the freeholders of Pawlingstown elected men like Wheeler and Coons to public office—men of such pronounced Whig loyalties. However, in 1776, the year the rebellion caught fire, Jeremiah French served as supervisor of the town and was paid twelve shillings for four days work. This was the same French who had petitioned the colony for two thousand acres of Preston Mountain for a glebe for the Episcopal Church. He was a wealthy Tory. In 1781, a newspaper said of him:[19]

Made their escape from the guard at Dover, Dutchess County, about the 25th of January ult. Two notorious villains, viz. Jeremiah French and William Draper, taken into custody for harboring, entertaining and concealing emissaries from the British; who it is not doubted, were either spies, recruiting-officers or horse-thieves, as several person went off with a number of stolen horses about that time....

Whoever takes up and secures said persons so that they may be brought to justice, shall receive Five Hundred Dollars reward for French and two hundred for Draper.

Zebulon Seaman, Lieut.[20]

Even before Pawlingstown paid French for his services as supervisor in 1776, he was considered dangerous to the Revolution's cause. That year, a Dutchess County committee, appointed to adopt measures to protect against Loyalists, included him in a list of men to be detained and shipped off to captivity in New Hampshire. While he faced deportation, his wife Hannah died in October 1776.

The citizens who elected Jeremiah French as supervisor probably knew his politics when they voted for him. The election of men on both sides of the fight suggests that the balance between Whig and Tory in the area was close. French was apparently welcome, for when the war ended, he returned to Dover from Vermont and died on his farm at Dover Furnace in 1793.[21]

Washington's army returned to Dutchess County in 1778. The soldiers camped for the winter in Pawlingstown, most of them on Quaker Hill. The decision to locate here arose from several factors: uncertainty as to the movements and intent of the British; anticipation of the arrival of the French fleet at Rhode Island; and the necessity of feeding and housing thousands of American troops through another winter. Quaker Hill seemed to offer a safe harbor from which to move if necessary. Washington and his officers commandeered quarters at various farmhouses on the hill and elsewhere. They took over the Oblong Meetinghouse as a hospital for the sick and wounded.[22]

The Friends extended a cold welcome to the soldiers. The Quakers were pacifists, but their neighbors believed they were Tories. The colonists had questioned their loyalties ever since the French and Indian War, when militia had confiscated Quaker livestock for failure to give military service. During the Revolution, the Friends never resisted the American soldiers, but they refused to help them. The members of the Oblong Meeting gave no aid to the convalescents there.

On Quaker Hill, being a Tory was a serious matter. The issues of the rebellion fostered violence there, even murder. In southern Dutchess County, everyone knew of the depredations of the "cowboys" and "skinners," the paramilitaries of Westchester County. Robert Rogers, the hero of the French and Indian War, commanded a Tory unit in Westchester. Encounters between Tories and Patriots engendered real fear.[23]

In the fall of 1776, when Jeremiah French and fifty-one other suspected Tories were shipped to New Hampshire for safekeeping, John Wheeler and Ephraim Wheeler were among them. They were related to Valentine; possibly they were his sons. Nevertheless, Valentine Wheeler maintained his enthusiasm for the Rebel cause. In July 1777, he presented a statement to the board:

Lieut. Wheeler produced a Bill of the Expence of the detachments of

Militia of capt. Chamberlayne's & Coon's Companies persuing and apprehending Delinquents and a Bill of the Expence of the Guard conducting Drink water to this place. . . .[25]

No battles were fought near Preston Mountain. So far as is known, no generals or other luminaries visited there. Only one Mountain soldier, Abel Rust, fought outside New York. Despite the presence of a handful of Tory sympathizers, most of the settlers were Patriots. When the war ended, the two sides returned to living side by side. Less than a year later, on August 11, 1782, Captain Valentine Wheeler died at age forty-one of unknown causes. He left a widow, Sarah, sons, Ephraim, John, and Josiah, and a daughter, Catherine. Valentine signed his will the day before he died.

> I, Valentine Wheeler, being sensible that it is appointed for all men once to die, and after death to come to Judgement, being sensible of my own frailty and mortality, would now, whilst I am in perfect sense, make this my last will and Testament. I leave to my wife the use of the home farm where I now live until my son Josiah of age, and after that the use of one-third. I leave to my son Josiah all my home farm after his mother's decease. I leave to my son Ephraim the farm where he now lives, lying on the mountain, beginning at the road on the top of the mountain, and all south as the road runs to the bog meadow, and as far south as my land goes. I leave to my son John the farm where Adam Coon now lives, running south as far as my land goes to John Bolt's land, and then a straight line to the top of the bald mountain, from thence to the French Doctor's former line. I leave to my daughter, Catherine Wheeler, the lot of land where Johannes Coon now lives, running from the top of the bald mountain south to Justice Mathew's land, from thence to the Connecticut line.[26]

If Valentine's sons Ephraim and John were Tories, and if his relative Adam Coon was a Tory, he forgave them all. The primitive descriptions of the land devised to his children make it difficult to determine the exact boundaries of the farms. But they were all on the Mountain, probably contiguous, and stretched from the Connecticut line to what is now Crane Pond. The farm devised to John has been discussed previously. Daughter Catherine inherited a wild piece of land east of the bald mountain. In a few years, a black family headed by Michael Jackson owned or occupied Catherine's land.

Chapter Seven
"Worthless Continental Money"

By 1783, Abel Rust, Justice Mathews, Phineas and Enoch Philleo, and all the surviving soldiers of the Revolution, came home. They had given up a large portion of their lives. Back on their farms, fields remained uncleared, walls unbuilt, farm buildings not started. The farms required unstinting labor. None of the Preston Mountain people inherited a farm. They all settled raw land and created their own farms. But they had just sacrificed seven years of their lives—seven years of labor not done.

Enoch Philleo returned to his wife Sarah at their crude dwelling on the Mountain. By 1783, they had three small sons; others would follow quickly. Surprisingly, Enoch's sister Esther married the Tory William Bradshaw, around 1785. Bradshaw was more than a sympathizer with the Loyalist cause; he actually fought on the side of the Tories. Like thousands of others who took the king's side, he moved to Nova Scotia late in the war. His nephew, Calvin Philleo (Enoch and Sarah's son) later said of him:

> He was a Tory in the Revolution, fought under the British flag, received three hundred acres of land as bounty at Nova Scotia at the close of the war, the prejudices were so against the Tories, but he eventually returned to his family.[1]

When Bradshaw returned, he and Esther set up housekeeping just up the hill from Enoch and Sarah. Their dwelling sat up high along the state line, just north of "Preston Hill." They rented fifty acres from Abel Harrington. Their property was referred to in later deeds as

Revolutionary War Veterans

POVERTY WAS THE COMMON LOT of most Revolutionary War veterans immediately after the war. There were no government hospitals to care for the wounded or sick, no Veterans Administration for the widows and children, and no GI Bill of Rights to educate the soldiers and make their lives better. One veteran, Joseph Plumb Martin described what faced the returning soldier:

> Starved, ragged, and meagre, not a cent to help themselves with, and no means or method in view to remedy or alleviate their condition; this was appalling in the extreme. All that they could do was to make a virtue of necessity and face the threatening evils with the same resolution and fortitude that they had for so long a time faced the enemy in the field.[2]

Joseph Plumb Martin served throughout the war, understanding when he enlisted that he would be paid "six dollars and two-thirds" each month. The army ceased paying him in 1777 and, with the exception of one month's pay in 1781, he never received another cent for his service. Martin concluded the narrative of his war experience with pages of bitter rebuke for his country's treatment of the veterans.[3]

One of the few things the government did for the veterans was to open up large tracts of land for veterans to settle. Some land, known as "bounty land," became available to veterans free or cheap. Joseph Plumb Martin considered moving up there, to "the western parts of the State of New York, where there was plenty of good land to be had as cheap as the Irishman's potatoes. . . ." The lure of these western lands struck the Preston Mountain veterans too, but only after many years of poverty on the Mountain.[4]

"William Bradshaw lands." Today, there is no physical evidence that people ever lived at this site; the Bradshaw homestead was probably as simple as the Philleos'.[5]

Despite having fought for opposite causes, William and Enoch socialized together. Calvin Philleo wrote that he remembered his father (Enoch) and his uncle (Bradshaw) getting together for talks. "Often have I heard them tell their war stories together."[6]

There was bitterness though. Calvin, who became a preacher, didn't spare his uncle: "He [William Bradshaw] was well paid for his treachery while my father received only worthless continental money."[7]

The Bradshaws had three children: Electa, Sabra (also known as Zaccheus), and Zachariah. In an age of biblical names for children, the Bradshaws outdid their neighbors. William lived to be over seventy-seven years of age and he died on the Mountain after 1837.[8]

The remainder of Phineas Philleo's life presents a small mystery. The family genealogy reports that he died of consumption in 1789 and that his widow, Silence, remarried Luke Wolcott's son Thomas in 1790. But the 1790 census shows Phineas living on the Mountain, the head of a family of eleven.[9]

In 1785, Sergent Abel Rust purchased, from Hendrick Winegar of Kent, a sawmill on one acre. The site was just east of the state line at the outlet of "Duck Pond" on the stream referred to in the deed as "the Sawmill Brook which comes from the mountain. . .located. . .south of the rattlesnake den."[10] It seems that Abel's peers respected him. The hill north of his home and sawmill became known as "Abel Rust Mountain."[11]

In January 1818, Abel Rust sold his home and sawmill to Martin Preston and his youngest son, John Preston II. Abel and his wife moved west (together with several neighbors from Preston Mountain) to Russia, New York, north of Utica. In his pension application, made when he was sixty-seven years old, Abel reported owning personal property worth $38.63. He declared, "Old age and infirmitis [sic] render it impossible for me to support myself and my wife by hand labor."[12, 13]

But he was not embittered by his poverty, and he was proud of his war service. The Rust family genealogy says, "Sgt. Abel Rust served under Gen. George Washington, and when he was very old he amused the younger folks with stories of his hardships during the war."[14]

By 1786, twenty years after Martin Preston first moved to the Mountain, twenty to twenty-five families lived there. None of them had yet recorded a deed for one jot of Preston Mountain. Under the law, none of them had perfected title to the land they worked and occupied. They knew their claims were uncertain. An event of 1786 demonstrated this fact. On September 7, 1786, forty-one men signed a petition to the New York State Legislature. Enoch Philleo then hand carried the petition to the legislature. It read:

> Whereas your Excellency's humble petitioners having settled on Certain Vacant lands situate on the Oblong in Pawling's Precinct being protracted by a scale of twenty chains to one inch by Nathan Soule, the number of acres is three thousand four hundred and twenty acres. Whereas your Excellency's humble petitioners humbly prays that his Excellency or the commissioners of the land office might inspect the map Which we have got of our land and that will give you a [illegible] description of the bounds. This we have sent by the bearer, Enoch Philleo.[15]

By 1786, Pawling was a town, no longer the precinct subdivision called Pawlingstown in Beekman's Patent. The forty-one men were proud new citizens of the United States. Yet, they continually referred to themselves as "humble." Perhaps this was a meaningless formality of contemporary legal documents. Perhaps it meant something else.

The document on file in the New York Land Papers appears to have been written by, and all the signatures signed by, one or two persons. If an attorney prepared it, he was not identified. Later documents demonstrate that many of the purported signers were illiterate and could not sign their own names; yet all forty-one signatures appear on the document without the customary "x" for "his mark." It's possible that the filed document is a transcript, and not the original document. But there is more that is strange about the 1786 petition.

The petition is as remarkable for what it does not say as for its content. It does not claim that the signers owned the land, or that they held title by virtue of grants, as Martin Preston's earlier petition had claimed. In fact, the signers refer to their interests only as "having set-tled on certain vacant lands..."[16] and as "proprietors of the land." There is no recitation of the history or longevity of their occupancy; in fact, there seems to be no effort made to convince the legislature of the justice of their claims.

The land involved lay south of the Rogers and Tonkrite Patent. It encompassed all the remaining lands of the Hoveout except the tracts William Smith and James Brown claimed in 1752 (see Chapter Three), which were specifically excepted and shown on Soule's map. These exceptions were peculiar because Martin, Timothy, and David Pre-ston, and Simeon Cummins (and probably several others) had been farming these tracts for decades.

There is also a suggestion of haste about the petition. There is no claim that Nathan Soule actually surveyed this land, only that he pro-tracted the acreage, perhaps based on an earlier map. Nathan was the surveyor who ran the Connecticut line and the person Ambrose Ben-son's daughter ordered off the land. Nathan's father, George Soule, and father-in-law, Nathan Birdsall, were also surveyors. Likely, Nathan Soule had the records to make a survey of the land described in the petition.

Enoch Philleo hand delivered the petition, probably riding seven-ty-five miles on horseback to Manhattan. There may have been no other effective way to deliver the petition without a postal service. Enoch was a vigorous and loyal soldier. He was probably the logical choice for the job. It is curious that the petition itself refers Enoch as the one who delivered it.

The petitioners may have thought that their efforts would improve their position as freeholders on the Mountain. Perhaps some official had promised them results if they made the application, maybe even imposing a time limit. Whatever the circumstances, the petition was artlessly drawn, hastily mapped, and quickly delivered by an unso-phisticated, even crude, yeoman. There is no record that the govern-ment of New York ever responded to the petition. But it is clear evi-dence that the forty-one men knew their hold on the Mountain was tenuous.

Even this did not slow the growth of the community. The census

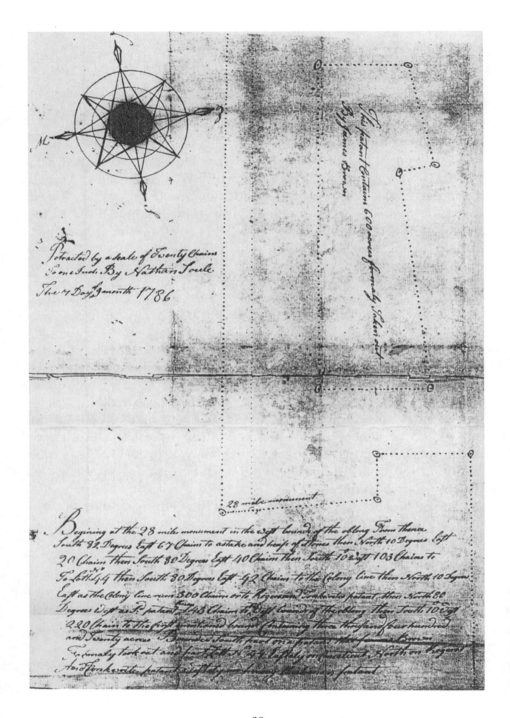

Protracted by a scale of Twenty Chains
To one Inch By Nathan Soule
The 7 Day 3 month 1786

This patent Contains 6000 acres formerly Salem act
By James Brown

28 mile monument

Begining at the 28 mile monument in the west bound of the obbery From thence
South 82 Degrees East 67 Chains to a stake and heap of stones then North 10 Degrees East
20 Chains then South 80 Degrees East 40 Chains then South 10 West 103 Chains to
To Lott 44 then South 80 Degrees East 92 Chains to the Colony Line then North 10 Degrees
East as the Colony Line runs 300 Chains or to Rozensand Tunheated patent then North 80
Degrees West as P. patent 148 Chains to West bound of the obbery then South 10 East
220 Chain to the first mentioned bound Containing three thousand six hundred
and Twenty acres

80

of 1790, the first census of the United States, reported twenty-five households on the Mountain—one hundred forty-three persons. Two other families may have lived there. These were big families; households with seven, nine, or eleven persons were the rule. Women and children were numerous, but there were only thirty-two adult males (over age sixteen) in the population.

The 1790 census is a list of names of adult male heads of household alongside columns enumerating (in order): the number of free white males over sixteen; the number of free white males under sixteen; the number of free white females of all ages; the number of "all other free persons;" and the number of slaves. Native Americans were not intended to be included in the census.

Volume I of Frank Doherty's *Settlers of the Beekman Patent* describes the manner in which the census is taken, noting that it was similar to the method used for the census taken for the Articles of Association of 1775 (for which the Pawling/Dover records have not survived). In that census Doherty writes: "The men carrying the lists went up and down the roads and had the residents sign as they came upon them."[17]

When the 1790 census was published, the inhabitants of Dover/Pawling were listed roughly according to the neighborhood where they lived, and not alphabetically. Therefore, if William Bradshaw was listed between Samuel Phillow (Philleo) and Justus Mathews (and he was), one could assume that Bradshaw's home was located between those of Phillow and Mathews along some road or path. The assumption is not without risk, however; Samuel Phillow might have lived at the end of some road in a totally different area of the community.

The majority of the Preston Mountain inhabitants are enumerated together on page eighty-eight of the published census, beginning with Joseph Eagard (Agard) and ending with Daniel Roberts. Two families, those of Richard Gillet and Luke Wolcott, appear together on page eighty-seven. This may mean, of course, that they were not on the Mountain in 1790, or it may mean that the census taker made a second trip to find them.

The census provides a snapshot of the families. Enoch and Sarah

Facing page: Nathan Soule's map for the 1786 petition showing tract claimed by William Smith and James Brown previously settled by the Prestons.

Philleo had four young sons and a daughter. The Bradshaw's home contained another female, probably their daughter, Electa. John Bolt and his wife lived alone. A young boy appears in the home of Gideon and Elizabeth Kenaday (Kennedy); he probably didn't survive because their son Alan wasn't born until 1794. David and Margery Preston, too, made a home for a young boy. Perhaps he was someone else's child, or he may have died young, for David and Margery died with no children surviving them. Simeon Cummins had a household of nine with three young boys. Martin and Rebecca Preston (Martin was then fifty) still supported four children, three females and their youngest son, John II. Phineas Phillow appears with a family of eleven, though his family genealogy says he died in 1789.

Slavery still existed in New York State in 1790. In Pawling there were forty-five slaves counted in nineteen homes. Luke Woolcot kept a slave, as did Martin Preston's brother Ebenezer. Ebenezer's son Ebenezer Jr. kept a person counted as "other free person," probably an African American servant.

There were fifteen households in Pawling in which all the inhabitants were counted as "all other free persons." These people, seventy in number, were freed slaves who were either tenants or freeholders in their own right. The largest such family was that of London Hill. Eight people in Hill's household lived on one hundred acres of Preston Mountain along the Connecticut border between Justus Mathews and John Bolt. London Hill was the pioneer of a small community of freed slaves who settled on the Mountain.

Chapter Eight
"All Other Free People"

THE NEW NATION CELEBRATED LIBERTY—for white men, not for women, children, Indians, or African Americans. In the United States, a father controlled his children's lives; a husband ruled his wife. Indians and African Americans trailed all the rest in the quest for rights. The Revolution began the journey to freedom for all.

> One obvious dependency the revolutionaries did not completely abolish was that of nearly a half million Afro-American slaves, and their failure to do so, amidst all their high-blown talk of liberty, makes them seem inconsistent and hypocritical in our eyes. Yet it is important to realize that the Revolution suddenly and effectively ended the cultural climate that had allowed slavery, as well as other forms of bondage and unfreedom, to exist throughout the colonial period without serious challenge. With the revolutionary movement, black slavery became excruciatingly conspicuous in a way that it had not been in the older monarchical society with its many calibrations and degrees of unfreedom; and Americans in 1775-76 began attacking it with a vehemence that was inconceivable earlier.[1]

The Quakers of the Oblong Meeting attacked slavery even earlier than 1775. In 1760, John Woolman, the great antislavery preacher of the Friends, in his epic journey through the American colonies, spoke to the Oblong Meeting. In 1767, the seeds of his preaching had sprouted.

> The Quakers who were prominent in Pawling were among the first to speak out against slavery. As early as 1755 the Quakers had taken a stand against trading in slaves and by 1767 the Oblong Meeting sent a notice to the Quarterly Meeting at Purchase in which they objected to even the holding of slaves obtained through inheri-

tance. . . .

In 1769 the Oblong Meeting on Quaker Hill became the first Meeting to free slaves as an action of the Body of the Meeting.[2]

By 1777, the Oblong Quakers believed that all the slaves that their members had owned had been freed. No statute governed the manumission of slaves at that time. Their own scruples motivated them, and they felt obliged to look after their former bondsmen, once freed. They referred to this obligation as "settling" with the freedmen.

Through the post-Revolution years, the minutes of the Oblong Meeting repeatedly refer to members settling with their former slaves. On the twelfth day of the fourth month of 1784:

> The Friends appointed on account of Negroes sett free made report that they don't find but Two Friends who have not made settlement with the Negroes and it appears the occasion is the remote situation of the Negroes from the friends who sett them free.[3]

Though the meeting encouraged such settlement, even appointed a committee to monitor the progress, the minutes are silent about the nature of settlements. Did the Quakers offer cash or land or provisions? The meeting minutes do not say.

London Hill and his family of eight lived a morning's ride from the Oblong Meetinghouse—close enough to receive a settlement. Adjoining deeds place his farm near the Connecticut line, not far north of the farm of the Tory William Bradshaw. Frank Doherty writes in *Settlers of the Beekman Patent*: "London Hill was probably a slave in the family of Caleb Hill of Dover and freed after the Revolution." Caleb Hill came late to Quakerism, joining the meeting in 1777. Caleb's daughter, Bethany or Bethania, married Ebenezer Soule in 1794, and they settled on Preston Mountain west of James Agard's farm. Perhaps out of respect, perhaps out of fear, London and Grace Hill named one of their sons, Caleb.[4]

As London Hill's children matured and married, their father held a tenuous grip on his Preston Mountain land. Like all his white neighbors, he never recorded a deed for his land. Later deeds referred to his place as "lands of London Hill," so he was at least reputed to own the farm.

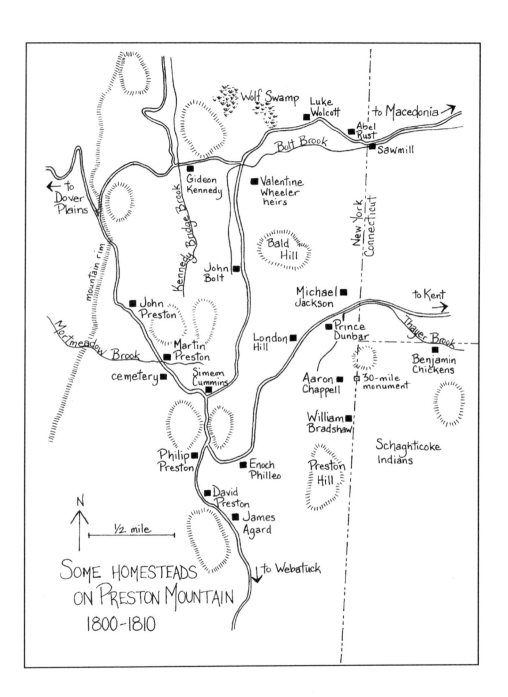

Wolf Swamp

Luke
Wolcott

to Macedonia →

Abel
Rust

Sawmill

Bolt Brook

← to
Dover
Plains

Gideon
Kennedy

Valentine
Wheeler
heirs

New York
Connecticut

Kennedy Bridge Brook

Bald
Hill

mountain rim

John
Bolt

John
Preston

Michael
Jackson

to Kent →

Thayer Brook

Prince
Dunbar

Nortmeadow Brook

Martin
Preston

London
Hill

Benjamin
Chickens

cemetery

Simeon
Cummins

Aaron
Chappell

⊡ 30-mile
monument

William
Bradshaw

Philip
Preston

Enoch
Philleo

Preston
Hill

Schaghticoke
Indians

N

↑

½ mile

David
Preston

James
Agard

↓ to Webatuck

SOME HOMESTEADS
ON PRESTON MOUNTAIN
1800-1810

85

"Governor of the Blacks"

HILL'S SON, LONDON HILL JR., married a woman named Liza Shoggum in Sharon, Connecticut, on July 8, 1798. They lived near his father according to the 1800 census. Liza was probably also known as Elizabeth Chaugham of Sharon, either a daughter or granddaughter of Molly and James Chaugham. Molly was an English woman—James a Narragansett Indian. Their story was told in *A Village of Outcasts*, by Kenneth L. Feder. The legend of Molly Barber told that she was the daughter of Peter Barber, "the richest man" living in Wethersfield, Connecticut. She wished to marry her sweetheart, but her father disapproved of him. The story was that Molly told her father that if he opposed her marriage, she would marry the first man who asked for her hand. Peter was adamant. So Molly ran off with his gardener, the Narragansett Indian James Chaugham.[5]

Molly and James lived for a time with Indians near Canton, Connecticut. When Peter Barber sent lawmen looking for his daughter the couple fled into the hills in Barkhamstead. They built a home on the slopes of Ragged Mountain overlooking the Farmington River, and there they started a family. In later years, a small community of all three races formed around the Chaugham's home. It was known as "the Lighthouse" because it was the only light seen during the long dark trip through that section of the Farmington Valley.

After James died around 1790, Molly moved to Sharon, where she bought land. Her son Samuel and daughter Elizabeth lived there. During the first decade of the nineteenth century, she moved back to the Lighthouse, where she lived until her death. The community remained on Ragged Mountain until late in the century when the residents disappeared. Some of the Chaughams moved to Kent. Only cellar holes remain at the Lighthouse.[6]

Meanwhile, Liza's brother-in-law Caleb Hill encountered

domestic problems with a woman (whose name was not recorded) who deserted him. Caleb sought the services of Kent lawyer
Barzillai Slosson:

> Slosson, so far as the daybook specifies, was directly
> engaged in a case of domestic trouble but once, and then,
> curiously enough, the case concerned a negro and his "pre-
> tended wife." The freedmen could—and usually did—refer
> such disputes to the "Governor of the Blacks" for settlement,
> but when Caleb Hill began to feel himself aggrieved at the
> desertion of his "pretended wife" he appealed to the white
> man's law and engaged Barzillai Slosson.[7]

> Slosson failed to report what outcome he obtained for Caleb,
> but he noted that he was compelled to sue the African American
> man for his fee, and he collected three shillings, fourpence. The
> identity of the "Governor of the Blacks" remained a mystery as
> well.

By 1800, several free African Americans lived near London Hill.
Many of them were relatives. Aaron Chapel (also spelled Chappell
and Chapell), born in 1749, built a home along the state line within
sight of the old thirty-mile monument from the original Oblong survey. Aaron's son, Aaron Jr. married London's daughter Queen.

Aaron had married a woman named Martha Obadiah in 1774. She
must have died young, because he subsequently married Hagar, a
woman named for the slave of the Old Testament Abraham. It is
unknown whether Aaron and Hagar had ever been slaves, and, if so,
who owned them. In any event, Aaron Chapel came to stay when he
moved to Preston Mountain. Aaron built a home with a stone cellar,
and substantial walls fenced his fields. Someone surveyed his farm; a
metes and bounds description of it existed by the time of his death in
1831. He also acquired eighty-seven acres in Kent adjacent to his New
York farm. The Kent land was located where Chapel Pond now appears on the topographic map.

London Hill's daughter Ruth married a free African American
man named Prince Dunbar (his surname appears in some census

records as "Dunbarack"). In 1800, Ruth and Prince lived somewhere between Aaron Chapel and London Hill Sr. There were seven other free persons living in their household according to the 1800 census, suggesting that Ruth and Prince had been married for several years by then. Frank Doherty wrote: "William Dunbar was probably the previous owner of Prince Dunbar an apparently freed slave." William Dunbar was a resident of Pawlingstown and a Revolutionary War veteran.[8]

Prince Dunbar was the first settler on Preston Mountain to record a deed for his land. On September 16, 1801, Nathan Soul (Soule) and Sarah, his wife, of Pawlingstown, for a consideration of ninety-five dollars, deeded sixty acres of land to Prince Dunbar. This is described partially as follows: "Beginning at Aron [sic] Chapel's northeast corner on the line dividing the States. . . ." The description ended, "and is part of the hoveout."[9]

Thomas, the Soule's son, and Enoch Philleo, the minuteman who was a nearby neighbor, witnessed the deed. The deed suggests that Prince was welcome on the Mountain, because Enoch witnessed it and he was a white man.

Nathan Soule was the land surveyor who mapped the lands for the signers of the 1786 petition and the same man who surveyed the state line near Ambrose Benson's farm. Soule owned a mill on the north bank of the TenMile River at the state line. In 1791, Pawlingstown raised a tax of twenty-six pounds to construct a bridge across the river at Nathan's mill, calling it "Soul's Bridge." Soule was a prominent member of the Oblong Friends Meeting, a member of its school's committee, and one of the trustees who owned the Preparative Meeting House at Webatuck. Sarah Soule's father, Nathan Birdsall, was also a surveyor (as was Nathan's father, George) and one of the first settlers of Quaker Hill.[10]

Perhaps the Soules deeded the land to Dunbar as part of the Quakers' settlement with a freed African American. Or it may have been simply a business transaction. The deed recites that Prince paid ninety-five dollars for the land, the place where he already resided. There is no record of how the Soules acquired the land. Whatever the true nature of the transaction, the Soules made Prince Dunbar a specific and highly unusual promise in the deed:

Nathan Soul do forever warrant and defend all said tract unto Prince Dunbar his heirs and assigns forever and do furthermore warrant and defend all said premises with every privilege thereunto belonging from Abraham Fuller of Kent and his heirs forever unto Prince Dunbar and his heirs forever. . . .[11]

Warranties and covenants of title were usual and customary in early New York deeds; but a warranty against the claims of a particular individual was highly unusual. What claim did Abraham Fuller of Kent make on Dunbar's farm? There was no recorded claim.

Abraham Fuller was a prominent Kent citizen. Born in 1737, he served as a captain in the Connecticut Militia during the Revolution, and he was known locally as "Captain Fuller." The town of Kent appointed him to committees to build and rebuild the bridge over the Housatonic, which was often taken out by spring floods. He and his wife, Lydia, were members of the Kent Congregational Church.[12]

Fuller was also the "Overseer of the Scatacooks." For over a century, the General Assembly of Connecticut appointed a Kent man to serve as overseer for the Indians to look after their interests and to conduct business on their behalf. Captain Fuller held the job for a quarter century, until 1801.[12]

The Scatacooks' land extended north along the state line on Preston Mountain as far as Thayer Brook. Prince Dunbar's eastern neighbor was either the Scatacooks or Abraham Fuller, but it amounted to the same thing because Fuller represented the Indians. Fuller never made any public claim to the Dunbar's land. Prince and his heirs held the farm for twenty-five years after 1801. His Scatacook neighbors were not so fortunate. Abraham Fuller, as their overseer, sold off their lands piecemeal during his tenure. This fact could not have escaped Nathan Soule, who was also a landowner in Kent.

Soon, another African American family appeared on the Mountain. Michael Jackson settled along the state line just north of Prince Dunbar. Jackson's next neighbor to the north was John Preston II.

Thus, a small community of African American freemen and their families assembled alongside the white settlers of Preston Mountain. Such African American settlements were common in the early nineteenth century. Another such group grew along the Dover-Amenia line and was known as the "Negro Corner." Most of these people had been recently freed from slavery; few of them had the resources or the support for survival. To a large extent, their success depended on the acceptance they found from the people around them.[14]

Looking at a topographical map today, the sites of the Jackson, Dunbar, Hill, and Chapel farms seem remote. There are, today, no roads anywhere near them. It is tempting to think that because these people were African Americans, they settled as far away from society as possible. But, in 1801, "the old road to Kent" curved through the Hill and Dunbar farms and just down the hill from the Chapel farm. If their white neighbors wished to travel to Kent (and that is where they sold charcoal and traded for provisions), they passed the homes of their African American neighbors. In fact, the African American families lived closer to whatever amenities Kent offered than did the white farmers.

Another look at the topographical map suggests that the land the freedmen occupied might have been the poorest available. Their farms were on the highest hills, often several hundred feet higher than their neighbors. However, like nearby Quaker Hill and Chestnut Ridge, some of the best farmland lay on the tops of the hills; the glaciers had deposited fertile soil there. The Preston Mountain farms were assessed and recorded in the "Tax List or Assessment Roll of Pawlingstown in the County of Dutchess for the year 1801." It reflected that the African American families owned land comparable to, or even better than, their neighbors. Some of the land assessments follow:

James Agard	$ 446.
Aaron Chapel	319.0
Philip Preston	230.0
London Hill	350.0
Enoch Philleo	160.0

The African American families and many of their white neighbors were clearly very poor, but some of their neighbors owned more land, or more valuable land.

John Bolt	$ 973.00
Simeon Cummins	622.00
Timothy Preston	834.00
Obadiah Preston	780.00

Martin Preston owned land that exceeded the value of his Mountain neighbors' land. With almost a square mile in his name, Martin's assessment was $2,318.00. Still, Martin was far from being the richest man in town. He ranked eighty-ninth on the list in terms of the size of his assessment.[15]

In 1807, the town known as Pawlingstown became two towns, Pawling on the south and Dover on the north. On April 9, 1807, the freeholders of Dover met for the first time as citizens at a town meeting at John Preston's tavern (now Old Drover's Inn). The town meeting was a New England tradition; it brought together all the men eligible to vote for a day of citizenship, socializing, eating, and drinking. In April, it was too cold to plant and too muddy to cut timber.

The meeting elected a town supervisor, town clerk, seven fence viewers, five constables, six pound-keepers, two overseers of the poor, and three appraisers; all of them signed oaths that the four justices of the peace witnessed. The meeting approved a tax of $450.00 for the support of the poor. They divided the town into twenty-one districts for the maintenance and repair of roads. They elected "overseers of the highways" for each district. On Preston Mountain, the first overseers were John Preston II and Aaron Chapel.[16]

For the next thirteen years, the men assembled each April at John Preston's tavern, and each year they elected an African American man as overseer of highways for the Preston Mountain district. Aaron Chapel held the job again in 1812 and 1815, though by then he was over seventy years old. Prince Dunbar and his sons Caleb and Robert, London Hill's sons Joseph and Henry (Harry), and Michael Jackson, all took their turns keeping the old road to Kent. But, after 1820, no person of color from Preston Mountain was ever again elected to town office.

It may be that levering boulders and filling quagmires on the roads was no honor—just free labor. If so, dozens of white men joined the African American men in the endeavor. The minutes of the meetings reflect that the nonwhite people enjoyed certain other rights in common with their fellow citizens. One such right was to record an "earmark." These were scars applied to livestock; they insured that if an animal strayed into a neighbor's woodlot, the beast's owner could claim it. In December 1807, Aaron Chapel recorded his mark, a half crop of the underside of the left ear and a whole crop on the right.

Earmarks measured the progress of husbandry in Dover. Stockmen with secure fences did not need to crop ears; their animals stayed home. On Preston Mountain, animals roamed, rooted, and foraged. Most of the animals in the valleys around the Mountain were confined. Forty percent of the earmarks recorded in Dover belonged to farmers on the Mountain. When the Prestons and the Chappells looked out at their pastures on a winter morning, someone else's hogs were probably rooting there. But they accepted these intrusions. Martin Preston's grandson Clark Preston recorded his first earmark in 1810, when he was twelve years old.[17]

For a time, white people and African Americans lived side-by-side on the Mountain in apparent harmony. The population of "all other free persons" varied from sixteen in 1800, to fifteen in 1810, to nineteen in 1820 and 1830. The freedmen were never isolated from their neighbors by location or race. Some of them were buried in the Mountain cemetery.

Martin Preston set aside an acre or so of his best farmland for a cemetery. Probably, dozens of people were interred there before any lasting monument was erected. Many flat, unmarked stones emerge from the soil, but the identity of the dead beneath will never be known. In 1813, James Agard died; his monument at the cemetery bears the first legible inscription. The next year, Lucy Chapel, Aaron's twenty-year-old daughter, died and was buried in the cemetery on the Preston farm. Aaron himself was buried beside Lucy after his death in 1831. But there are no other marked gravestones for nonwhites in this cemetery.

Certainly, between 1790 and 1831, several members of the Hill, Chapel, Dunbar, and Jackson families must have died. London Hill died in either 1804 or 1808 (the records conflict). Where were these people buried? There is a brief reference in the Benson family genealogy saying that, as of 1914, some people believed a "negro cemetery" existed on the old Hufcut farm on the Mountain. The old Hufcut farm of more than three hundred acres included all or most of what had been the farms of the free African Americans.[18]

A Preston Mountain gravestone without inscription.

During the 1790s, a Schaghticoke Indian named Benjamin Chickens established a homestead across the state border from African Americans, probably within hailing distance. His place was located at the northwest corner of the reservation. Samuel Orcutt's book, *The Indians of the Housatonic and Naugatuck Valleys*, quotes an unattributed source: "At this time (1801) Benjamin Chickens, a descendant of the old Captain Chickens was a careful and industrious farmer at this place."[19]

Benjamin himself, in a later petition to the General Assembly of Connecticut, reported what he had done. He claimed that in 1793 or 1794 he had, "gone on to the N.W. part of said land [The Schaghticoke lands along the New York border] at a distance from the residence of the other Indians of said tribe and had there build himself a small but Convenient House, had cleared up and fenced several Acres of said Land, and had Cultivated the same in such manner that a part thereof had become good meadow and pasture land and a part good plough land. . . ."[20]

Benjamin's farm was just northeast of where Chapel pond lies today and near where Thayer Brook begins its steep descent into the Housatonic Valley. The land he cleared and fenced was farmed by at least two families after him—the families of Michael Barley and Ezekiel Thayer. It was good farmland for the Mountain. But, in 1801, Benjamin Chickens was facing trouble.

Chapter Nine
The "Scatacooks"

THE NATIVE AMERICANS known as the Schaghticokes or Scata-cooks occupied the southeastern flank of the Mountain from the New York line east to the Housatonic River. The Mountain rises steeply behind their ancestral village; it is known here as "Schaghti-coke Mountain." The boundaries of their lands, which the Connecticut government held for them, shrank over time. When colonial settlers first appeared in Kent, the Schaghticokes' northerly boundary was a line between the Housatonic and the New York border near Thayer Brook. Today, their northerly boundary is two miles farther south. The "reservation" is a fraction of its original size.

The word "Schaghticoke" derives from the name "Pischgoch-ti-goch" an Algonquin word meaning, "where the waters meet." Pis-chgoch-ti-goch is where TenMile River empties into the Housatonic River. This old home site is now a designated campsite along the Appalachian Trail. As the English advanced, the Schaghticokes retreated north from Pishgoch-ti-goch, moving two miles along the west bank of the river to the place where the remnant of their land remains. Here, they established the settlement known as Schaghti-coke, built homes, and buried their dead in the little cemetery over-looking the river.[1]

The tribe's name reflects its history. It is spelled "Schaghticoke" today. In 1752, the General Assembly of Connecticut referred to the tribe as "Scatacooks." English speakers, ignorant of Indian words, spelled them phonetically. The Chickens' family name had nothing to do with poultry. It sounded like "chickens" to white men, but the word's meaning had fled.[2]

The last fluent speaker of the Schaghticoke tongue died in 1903, only a few months before the arrival of ethnologist Frank G. Speck in Kent. He reported sixteen Indians then living on the reservation. He was able to learn only twenty-three words of their language and three connected sentences. But for bad luck, Speck might have preserved some of their language and shed some light on the true history of the Schaghticokes.[3]

Instead, white historians who were generally unsympathetic to their subject have told the Schaghticoke story. For example, Francis Atwater's 1897 *History of Kent, Connecticut* says, "In 1801, the Scatacooks were reduced to thirty-five idle, intemperate beings, who cultivated only six acres of ground. Their land still amounted to twelve or fifteen hundred acres extending from the Housatonic to the New York line." Atwater credited the State Records, Volumes VI and VII for this information.[4]

Back in 1854, John W. DeForest, in *History of the Indians of Connecticut*, used the exact same quote. DeForest also attributed this material to Volumes VI and VII of the State Records.[5]

The true source of these allegations was Abraham Fuller, the overseer of the Schaghticokes in 1801. In a petition to the general assembly asking for authority to sell most of the Indians' lands, Fuller claimed: "that the number of said Indians is reduced to thirty-five who are reduced to idleness and intoxication and averse from Labour and do not pretend to cultivate more than Six Acres of their said land...." Fuller's petition does appear in the State Records.[6]

There existed no Indian voices to tell the condition of the Schaghticokes in 1801. Like their neighbors on Preston Mountain, the Indians were illiterate. White historians focused on the habits that the overseers reported; the Schaghticoke side of the story remained unreported.

By 1801, the Schaghticokes were a besieged and hounded people. They were the descendants of several lines of Native Americans, some from farther south in Connecticut, and some (perhaps) from the Mohican or Mahican peoples of nearby New York. There have been attempts at tracing their roots, but only a vague outline has emerged. Trudy Lamb Richmond described their society:

One factor that the native communities along the Housatonic River had in their favor was that they were all related. There were major village settlements such as those of the Paugussett people, who had several sites along the mouth of the river and inland as far as is now Derby and Shelton. The Pootatucks were located in the South-bury/Woodbury area and the Weanitocks who held the major Council Fire, were in New Milford. . . .

The Housatonic was well populated and there was a great deal of movement along its extensive shore.[7]

Indians in Connecticut first encountered large numbers of whites in the early 1600s. These meetings devastated the Indians. "The massacre of 400 Pequots at Mystic and the killing of at least another 600 in the Great Swamp within Paugussett territory had to create great emotional turmoil in the hearts of native people in the area."[8]

Some of the Pequots fled north. One of their leaders, Sassacus, escaped into New York with a small band of followers. There is a legend that they hid in a cavern in Dover known as the "Stone Church." When they felt safe, they moved on to the north, only to be captured and killed by the Mohawks, who sold Sassacus' scalp (or head) to the English.[9]

It is possible that other Pequots joined the Schaghticokes at Pish-goch-ti-goch, and, over the years, became part of the tribe.

During the 1637 Swamp Fight in Pequannock territory, some 60-70 Pequot warriors managed to escape and fled northwards. . . . It is probably that some of these escapees joined the Weanitoch Indians whose territory lay to the north of that of the Pequannock. Oral history among the Schaghticokes in the eighteenth and nineteenth century [sic] at least mentions traditions of Pequot ancestry.[10]

In 1855, a Schaghticoke woman, Eunice Mauwee, (more later on her) joined the Kent Congregational Church; her name appeared on the church rolls as "Eunice Mauwee, Last of the Pequots."

The Pequots provided a minor infusion into the tribal bloodstream at most. The immediate predecessors to the Schaghticokes were the Weanitocks of New Milford. Their chief was Waramaug. "Recorded history began for the Weanitocks about 1646 when Stephen Goodyear established a trading post on an island in [the] Housatonic river a few miles below the main settlement of the tribe."[11]

Colonization of the Weanitock territory began about 1670. Fifty years later, pressure from the Yankee settlers reached the breaking point.

> In 1736, finally, the Weanitock left their encroached lands in New Milford and settled at Schaghticoke on the west bank of the Housatonic River in present-day Kent, located in that part of the territory that was not (yet) threatened by white colonization.[12]

Three years later, the General Assembly of Connecticut opened Kent for settlement, and, by 1740, white men were probably clearing land across the river from the Indians. Chief Waramaug died in 1735. Leadership of the Schaghticokes passed to Gideon Mauwee.

> The people were fortunate because a new leader did emerge. His name was Mauwee or Hungry Bear. Like Waramaug, he had been a sagamore, a sub-chief. . . . For a long time it was Mauwee's vision and leadership abilities that enabled the people to come together. He welcomed other native peoples as they traveled up river looking for new homes and called out to relatives and friends to join him in the new place called Schaghticoke.[13]

About the same time, a group of German missionaries, the Moravians, began preaching to Mohican Indians in nearby colony of New York. At Shekomeko [south of Pine Plains], and Wechquadnach [Indian Pond, south of Millerton], these missionaries settled in or near Mohican villages. They converted many Indians to Christianity and they lived in peace with their neighbors. By 1743, the Moravians discovered the Schaghticokes.

> The outlet of Wechquadnach drains into Ten Mile, or Webatuck, which flows into the Housatonic, and above their junction, about two miles below Kent, Connecticut, was Patgatgoch (Scaticook), a third settlement composed mostly of "Wampanos" (Wampanoags), or "King Philip's Men," fugitives from still further east.[14]

DeCost Smith's assertion that the Schaghticokes were Wampanos or Wampanoags is one of the many attempts to trace the confusing background of the tribe. Wojchechowski's *Ethnohistory of the Paugussett*

Tribes makes some sense out of the relation between "Wampanos" and "Schaghticokes."

> In the writings of the Moravian missionaries the Schaghticoke ("Pachgatgoch") and the Potatuck Indians are collectively referred to as Wampano [citation omitted]. The above reference to the Wampano (Wampamo) language therefore suggests that the Schaghticoke and Potatuck spoke the same language. Furthermore, the community at Schaghticoke in the Moravian mission period already contained a sizeable number of Pequannock Indians, who had mostly arrived in the 1740s as migrants from the Redding area [citation omitted]. These Indians did not merge with the Schaghticoke until at least the 1760s [citation omitted]. The fact that the Moravian missionaries at Schaghticoke in their writings never mentioned the existence of linguistic diversity at Schaghticoke, suggests that the Pennaquock language too was basically identical to that of the Weanitock (Schaghticoke) Indians.[15]

Gideon Mauwee (Mauwehu) welcomed the Moravians, who lived with the Native Americans as part of their community. DeForest reported: "Mauwehu and about one hundred and twenty to one hundred fifty of his people were baptized. A church was built, and a flourishing congregation collected. An almost total reformation seemed be effected in the character of the Indians."[16]

But the wave of religious feeling that swept the Mohicans and the Schaghticokes provoked animosity from the white settlers in both Kent and Dover, for whom the Moravian version of Christianity was foreign. DeForest wrote that in Kent:

> This wide spread religious interest excited feelings of deep animosity among the rum sellers and dissolute characters of the surrounding district. They saw their gains at once cut off. And the Indians who had formerly been their best customers, now became temperate and saving. Reports were spread that the missionaries were providing the Indians with arms, and endeavouring [sic] to draw them into league with the French.[17]

Meanwhile, in Dover, an unnamed minister accused the Moravians:

That they had three thousand stand of arms and an ample supply of powder and ball hidden in their bark cabins, awaiting the opportune moment when they and their so-called "Christian Indians" would join the French in massacring the English, German and Dutch settlers.[18]

In both colonies the courts and the militia began to harass the Moravians. They were compelled to give military service in New York (though, like the Quakers, they were pacifists) and to give an oath of allegiance (though they could swear no oaths, only affirm the truth). The government forbade them to teach the Indians unless they complied. White settlers who distrusted and feared them surrounded the Schaghticokes and the Moravians. The struggle with the French added fuel to the fire, which a jealous clergy ignited. In 1746, some of the Moravians gave up and moved to the settlement at Bethlehem, Pennsylvania. A few Schaghticokes and Mohicans went with them, but a schism developed with the Indians.

The religious ferver among the Schaghticokes waned in time, when they discovered that the salvation offered by Moravian missionaries only concerned their souls and did not effectively extend to their bodies or their lands. By 1762 the Schaghticokes were indeed at low ebb.[19]

Their problems worsened when Connecticut added the lands west of the Housatonic to Kent in 1751. Then, the Mountain north of the Schaghticoke lands was opened for settlement. The Indians' land tempted the colonists. In 1757, the general assembly appointed a white overseer, Jabez Smith, to protect the Indians' interests. In 1760, their chief Gideon Mauwee died "on Schaghticoke Mountain at the age of seventy-three." The Schaghticokes were then dependent on their overseer.[20]

Captain Abraham Fuller was appointed overseer before 1777. He held the job until 1801. Fuller evidently believed that the Indians were best served if their lands were sold and the proceeds spent or invested by the overseer on behalf of his charges. He pursued this goal relentlessly. Below are synopses of two of Captain Fuller's "Memorials to the General Assembly."

In 1778, for authority to sell ten acres of the family of Warrups because the family was in indigent circumstances and the old squaw was blind, and to apply the avails thereof to the relief of said Indian family.[21]

In 1783, for authority to sell forty acres of unimproved land lying contiguous to the New York line, "so far out of the way of your Memorialist that great Encroachments are almost constantly made. . . whereby your Memorialist is put to great difficulty and inconvenience."[22]

By 1786, the Schaghticokes grew unhappy with Fuller's services. They complained to the general assembly, asking that someone look into the " disposition of their lands and the rents therof by Capt Abraham Fuller their present Conservator."[23] They also asked for a school for their children. The government appointed John Canfield, Esq., General Heman Swift, and Captain Simeon Smith to investigate the matter. DeForest reported the results of their work:

> They reported—that, so far from the Scatacooks being entitled to complain of their guardian they were actually indebted to him to the amount of sixteen shillings and six pence. The committee further stated that the lands were rented for only one year, and thus tenants were induced to exhaust them without any regard to their future fertility. They recommended that fifty acres should be allotted to each indian family, and that the rest should be leased to white farmers in terms of fifty years. As for the school, they reported that the children were so few in number, and "kept in such a wild savage way" that the thing would be useless. The report was approved by the General Assembly.[24]

This was the judgment of what was for Litchfield County a "blue-ribbon" committee. Canfield was a prominent Sharon attorney. He defended Colonel John Ashley in the landmark Massachusetts slave case, Brown and Bett vs. Ashley. General Heman Swift of Cornwall had been commander of the Second Connecticut Line in the Revolution, was promoted to brigadier general, and served on Washington's staff. They were highly respected men, but they clearly had no regard for Indian children.

Perhaps encouraged by the findings of the general assembly, Captain Fuller promoted further sales of Schaghticoke lands. In 1800, on his application, a committee informed the assembly that "there appeared to be a Debt due from said Skatacook Indians of about One hundred and twelve pounds and—it is expedient and necessary to sell so much of said Skatacook land as to pay said debt with the incident charges of sale."[25] The general assembly approved the sale of enough land, to be taken off at the southern end, to pay the debt.

There were other sales of the Indian lands during Abraham Fuller's tenure as overseer. In 1786, the Schaghticoke's neighbor Jacob Bull collected a debt from the "family of Warrups," specifically Eunice Warrups, who owned thirty acres of land. Fuller and Bull opined that the thirty acres would satisfy the debt, and the general assembly approved the sale.[26]

Captain Fuller saved his greatest accomplishment for last. In 1801, in the same memorial in which he accused the Indians of idleness and intoxication, Fuller asked the general assembly for authority to sell enough of the Indians' land to pay a debt of four hundred dollars. The debt was incurred because "the Indians have of late years been much afflicted with sickness." The general assembly voted that Heman Swift and John Talmadge be empowered to sell all the Scatacooks' lands lying north of a line drawn from the Housatonic, past "the Middle Gate, so called" to the state line.[27]

Probably, some Kent residents knew where the "Middle Gate, so called" was located; the Schaghticokes knew. Certainly Abraham Fuller knew. But it is doubtful that many other members of the General Assembly of Connecticut realized just how much of the Schaghticokes' land this resolution authorized to be sold. The sale disposed of 1,129 acres—at least two-thirds of their remaining land. The Indians lost all of their land north of the Middle Gate for a distance of about two miles. The proceeds of the sale were $4,326.66, more than ten times the sum needed to pay the $400.00 debt.[28]

Later, historians Atwater and DeForest reported that the sale proceeds were thirteen hundred pounds. While they both acknowledged that the sale was made to pay a debt of four hundred dollars, they still reported the sale price in pounds. This was despite the fact that the deeds of the three men who purchased the land recited each price in dollars. Thirteen hundred pounds does not sound like quite so much money as four thousand dollars.[29]

Ephraim Beardsley Jr., Dr. John Raymond, and Ebenezer Preston Jr. were the three purchasers. Dr. Raymond was the Kent physician who treated the Indians. Ebenezer Preston owned mills along TenMile River in Dover; he was also Martin Preston's nephew. Beardsley and Raymond acquired parcels along the Housatonic River and on the lower flanks of the Mountain. Preston purchased two miles of woods along the New York border at the top of the Mountain.

Raymond paid $1,600 for 159 acres. Beardsley paid $1,666 for 370 acres. Preston paid $1,000 for six hundred acres. Each man gave a mortgage back to the overseer for a portion of the purchase price. All three deeds were dated September 1, 1801, three months after the general assembly authorized the sale. The Indian land had to be surveyed and subdivided in order to create the deeds, all of which contained metes and bounds descriptions for most of the boundaries between the parcels. In addition, a surveyor had calculated the acreage of each parcel as reflected in the deeds. Only one boundary was left unde-fined—that between the parcels conveyed to Preston and Raymond. They entered into a boundary line agreement in 1805 in which they claimed to "have today perambulated the line between us."[30]

The northerly boundary of the lands sold adjoined lands Abraham Fuller owned. On October 13, 1801, the general assembly accepted his resignation as overseer for the Schaghticokes. Abel Beach became the new overseer. Beach owned land adjoining the southerly boundary of what remained of the Schaghticoke reservation.

Chapter Ten
The Scattering:
The United States in 1800

THE PEOPLE OF PRESTON MOUNTAIN lived in a rapidly changing nation; Americans were tired of the conditions of the past and they were flexing their muscles for the future. Many historians have written about the country's politics and its prominent leaders. Few have sketched a picture of the common people or the land. Henry Adams did so. His *The United States in 1800* was a snapshot of America.

Adams emphasized the primitive state of communication, transportation, and agriculture. It surprised him that any progress could occur under such conditions.

A postal service existed, but it was spread thin along major post roads and served only nine hundred post offices in the whole country. New York also had a public school system, but the state treasury was empty and the school system dwindled. There was no school on the mountain until 1820.[1]

Roads were primitive—maintained only haphazardly by private citizens. Commerce and civilization flourished along navigable waterways but declined in places distant from these streams.

> New York was still a frontier, and although the City was European in its age and habits, travelers needed to go few miles from the Hudson in order to find a wilderness like that of Ohio and Tennessee.[2]

Adams stressed that western New York was still a wilderness. " Buffalo was not laid out; Indian titles were not extinguished...Albany was still a Dutch city with some five thousand inhabitants."[3]

He compared the American farmer of 1800 with the Saxon farmer of a thousand years earlier and found remarkably little change. Both were illiterate, uninformed, and poor. "[N]either their houses, their clothing, their food and drink, their agricultural tools and methods, their stock, nor their habits were greatly altered or improved. . . ."[4]

Among the habits of the American people, Adams noted, was an unhealthy diet. "Salt pork three times a day was regarded as an essential part of American diet. . . . Thus the ordinary rural American was brought up on salt pork and Indian corn or rye; and the effect of this diet showed itself in dispepsia."[5]

After 1801, Preston Mountain families of all races began to leave the Mountain. New families replaced some of them: Cooks, Patchens, Griffens, and Ortons arrived on the mountain. Some families left their homesteads vacant. Economic factors played a major role in the emigration. The poorer families left while the wealthier stayed.

One of the first to go was the Schagticoke farmer, Benjamin Chickens. Abraham Fuller had included Benjamin's place in the northwestern corner of the tribe's lands in the sale to Ebenezer Preston Jr. for $1.66 per acre. In 1803, Chickens petitioned the General Assembly of Connecticut for redress for the loss of his farm. The general assembly voted to authorize the new overseer, Abel Beach, to pay Chickens the sum of one hundred dollars. According to the overseer's account book, Beach paid him one hundred dollars in 1804 from money he held in trust for the whole tribe.[6]

The United States census of 1800 showed Benjamin Chickens living in Pawlingstown, (later Dover), New York, among the Preston Mountain inhabitants. This may have been a census taker's error; Chicken's farm was close to the New York border. In any event, he was the only Native American ever to be counted among the settlers on Preston Mountain. How his neighbors responded to him is unknown.

Apparently, Benjamin Chickens intended to move to a home in New York State. In 1810, he again petitioned the general assembly:

That he owns a piece of land of about nineteen acres in said Kent, for which he gave one hundred dollars, and he is about to remove into the State of New York where he has purchased a farm of land, and that it is necessary he should sell his land in Kent, in order to make payment for his land in New York.[7]

The general assembly permitted him to sell his land to Asa Parks, "under the direction" of Abel Beach, and to pay for his farm in New York, also "under the direction of said Beach."[8]

In 1812, Benjamin Chickens and Abraham Rice attempted to sell a plot of land to John and Robert Wilson. Abraham Rice was an African American man and the son-in-law of Benjamin's neighbor Aaron Chappell. The Wilsons were in the iron business at Macedonia, where the parcel lay. But some official nullified the recorded deed, which was signed by Rice and marked "x" by Chickens. The official noted on it: "this deed is a quit claim is recorded where it ought not to be is therefore null and void."[9]

Ebenezer Preston Jr. had acquired Benjamin Chicken's Mountain farm. Ebenezer had the six hundred acres surveyed and subdivided into seven lots or parcels of varying acreages. In 1805, he sold the two most northerly parcels. Fifty acres went to Michael Barley of Kent for $200.00. Aaron Chappell of Pawlingstown bought eighty-seven acres for $328.00. Thus Ebenezer received $4.00 per acre and $3.77 per acre for land that he had paid $1.66 per acre for four years previously.

Chapel and Barley gave mortgages back to Preston, payable at the dwelling of Michael Barley in Kent. Aaron financed $266.00 of his purchase, meaning that he had $62.00 cash to put down. Barley gave three notes of $30.00 each. He later borrowed $42.00 from Martin Preston's son Timothy and mortgaged his fifty acres as security.[10]

Aaron Chapel's eighty-seven acres lay adjacent to his New York farm on the hillside sloping down to the swamp that would later become Chapel Pond. He owned more than one hundred forty acres on the Mountain.

Abel Beach continued the work of Abraham Fuller as overseer of the Schaghticokes. By 1805, he had loaned the proceeds from the 1801 land sale to Philonius Beardsley, Jabez Beardsley, Benjamin Benson, Dr. John Raymond, Gilead Hurd, John Hurd, and John Lain. Beach accounted for his expenditures as overseer. He paid himself twenty dollars each year. Dr. John Raymond received ten dollars each year for doctoring the Indians. Three dollars a year went to the owners of the cemetery where the Schaghticokes were buried for "use of the burying ground." The owners of the cemetery were Ephraim Beardsley Jr. and Dr. John Raymond. It's unclear when or why the Schaghticokes divested themselves of their cemetery. Beach also purchased goods for the Indians—shoes, blankets, and corn, and "one pint of gin for old Sarah."[11]

In 1811, Beach asked the general assembly for authority to sell "twenty acres— useless to said Indians." The land to be sold bordered the river. The assembly approved the sale.[12]

The same year, the general assembly appointed two lawyers "to examine, audit and adjust the accounts of the Scatacook tribe of Indians and to make their report thereon to this Assembly at their session in May annually." The auditors were Julius Caswell and Barzillai Slosson of Kent. Slosson, who died in 1813, left a manuscript history of Kent in which he set forth his opinion of the Schaghticokes: "The constant and universal habit of drunkenness among them has degraded them to a station but little superior to the beasts." Slosson probably disapproved the expenditure for Old Sarah's gin.[13]

Samuel Orcutt described the gradual scattering of the tribe to other places. Most of the Schaghticokes moved to work in the cities of Connecticut until, "in 1836 Eunice Mauwehu and two or three families were all that remained of the tribe at Scaticook." This was the same Eunice, "the Last of the Pequots," who joined the Kent Congregational Church. She died at Schaghticokes in 1860, age 104. Before she died she was interviewed by Myron B. Benton, who reported the following:[14]

> I have always been glad that I was so fortunate as to have an interview with Eunice Mauwee, where I saw her in her little cottage in Schaticook [sic] about the year 1859. This was a few months before her death. . .she related some incidents pertaining to her people. . . ."[15]

That is all Benton wrote. Whatever incidents Eunice Mauwee related to him went to his grave with him.

Scattered Families

IN THE YEARS AFTER 1808, several Preston Mountain families moved to Russia Corners in the town of Russia, Herkimer County, New York. Russia Corners is a crossroads along the old Military Road from Albany to Sackett's Harbor on Lake Ontario. It is on a high plateau overlooking the Mohawk Valley to the south and the Canada River Valley to the west. The plateau is actually the southwest corner of the Adirondacks. It must have seemed familiar to the folks from Preston Mountain—a high, rugged wilderness. But instead of white pines waving along the ridgetop, the dark, pointed shapes of larch and spruce marked the horizon. Instead of bouldery fields of thin soil, the farms of Russia Corners boasted a rich gravelly loam. Once cleared, Russia's fields were broad and unbroken. Paula Johnson, the Russia town historian wrote: "Prior to 1806, the entire area was virtual wilderness. There were only a few settlers and their homes were scattered."[16]

The Military Road served to open up the North Country and the Black River Valley to settlement.

> This road was the major pathway over which the great flow of people traveled to their new homes. It became a path of opportunity for local people with all sorts of services catering to travelers being established along it. as were new house and communities. Farmhouses remain today which resemble the early one and a half story saltboxes of early Massachussetts and Long Island from which a large number of early settlers came.[17]

The first emigrants from Preston Mountain to acquire land in Russia Corners were Abel and Darius Philleo, sons of Enoch and Sarah. They both recorded deeds in 1808, the same year the Military Road was opened across the plateau. Both Abel and Darius later served as soldiers in the War of 1812. It is possible they helped build the road before the war. "During the war of 1812 this road was used to supply the fort at Oswego on Lake Ontario. Troops were marched over it and chains carried north to close the St. Lawrence River to the British."[18]

Enoch and Sarah Philleo apparently followed their sons to Russia in 1810. They were counted twice in the federal census of that year, once on Preston Mountain and once in Russia. In subsequent years, three other Philleo sons, Calvin, Milton, and Bonaparte, owned land in Russia.

Soon, other Preston Mountain people followed the Philleos. Sergeant Abel Rust bought a farm there in 1818, probably on or near Buck Hill, a flank of the main plateau. The next year, Abel's sons, Philo, Julius, and Hiram, acquired land in town. Philo's wife, the former Lury Agard, brought her mother with them. Annah Judd Agard, Rebecca Preston's sister, is buried beside Philo and Lury Rust in the Hinckley Road Cemetery near Russia Corners. Annah's husband, James Agard, died in 1813 back in Dover.

Being related to the Agards was the common denominator of those who moved to Russia. Sarah Philleo was James Agard's sister. James and Annah's daughter Diadema, with her husband, Peter Roberts, and her father-in-law, Daniel Roberts, arrived in Herkimer County in 1817. There were several Roberts families living there, not all of whom were related to Daniel and Peter.

Ephraim and Edward Wheeler moved to Russia in 1807 and joined the Russia Union Church, a big, white-steepled meetinghouse that still stands at the junction of Russia Corners. The church records reflect that the Wheelers arrived from Amenia, New York, (the church was founded in 1818). Though the Wheelers' given names were the same as Valentine Wheeler's sons, these two men were not the sons of the Revolutionary War captain. A man named Simeon Commins lived in Russia at the same time, but it is unclear whether he was the Simeon Cummins who lived down the road from Martin Preston on the Mountain in Dover.

Abel Rust's son Hiram had a son named William P. Rust, who merited a short biography in the history of Herkimer County.

William P. Rust is a farmer and geologist and was born in Russia in 1827. He has for the past ten years been engaged in collecting and developing specimens of fossil remains from the Trenton rock and Utica slate, and science owes to him the discovery of many forms of life in the rocks unknown to it before. (William P. Rust owned a quarry). He collected a large series of the fossils of the Trenton limestone, and possesses one of the finest cabinets of trilobite specimens in the state. His grandfather, Abel Rust, a veteran of the Revolution, settled in this town in 1818, and died in 1842, age ninety-three years. His father, Hiram, was born in Kent, Connecticut, July 4, 1794, and came to this town with his parents. He, with many other settlers, witnessed the changes in their early home surroundings, from the log cabin and just cleared tract to the comfortable home and broad open fields.[19]

The two old Revolutionary War soldiers, Enoch Philleo and Abel Rust, both lie in the Hinckley Road Cemetery. Enoch Philleo's stone reports his death in 1827, age sixty-seven. That would have made him fifteen when he enlisted and cannot be correct. Abel Rust's name is spelled "Able" on his stone. The stone notes that he was a "soldier of the Revolution," and he died in 1847, age ninety-five.

The same cemetery contains the remains of Abel Rust's great-grandson, the second sergeant Abel Rust. He was born in 1830, and thus spent ample time with his great-grandfather, and, no doubt, took to heart the old soldier's war stories. The younger Abel Rust was killed in June 1864 at the beginning of Grant's siege of Petersburg, Virginia.

The family genealogy says that Enoch Philleo "died in the cornfield at Russia Corners, New York." He and Sarah never became wealthy. Their legacy was their sons. Born in the earth-floored cabin on Preston Mountain, several Philleo boys grew up to lead remarkable lives:

Martin, Abel, Darius, and Milton, all moved to Russia and all served in the War of 1812.

Calvin became a prominent Baptist minister whose "power over audiences was almost unequaled."

Luther lived to be at least eighty-six years old. "He was gifted with musical talent and began when a small boy to make violins with an old razor." He also built pianos and a planetarium. Luther "was said to be a genius."

Addison became a physician. He moved to Galena, Illinois, and founded a newspaper, the *Galenian*. He served as a surgeon during the Black Hawk War. He died of "intermittent fever" in 1841 at Tampa Bay, Florida.

Bonaparte graduated from the Medical College at Fairfield, New York, and practiced medicine in western New York.

Jefferson also became a physician, and he, too, practiced in Galena, Illinois. The Philleos' only daughter, Lucinda, died in infancy. If nothing else, the Philleos' sons inherited their father's energy and their mother's patience.[20]

In 1813, a mysterious illness struck the northeast. It was already widespread by the end of the war, and soldiers returning home may have spread it. Martin and Rebecca Preston's son-in-law Thomas Wolcott served in the war and returned to the Mountain. But, there were probably many sources of infection. James Agard, John Bolt II, Prince Dunbar, and Ebenezer Preston Jr. all died that year. Some thought the disease was typhus. The prevalence of the disease earned it the dread name, "the epidemic."

More bad luck soon followed the epidemic—a period of catastrophic weather. On September 23, 1815, a hurricane hammered New England, leveling trees by the millions from Long Island Sound to New Hampshire. The next year, 1816, has been called "Eighteen Hundred and froze to death." There was frost in every month of the year.

Vermont received a foot of snow on June 8. It was "the year of two winters."

For a generation, tales of rich, cheap land to the westward had tempted the less prosperous farm people. Now, with New England experiencing Arctic weather, could they be worse off in the Western Reserve? "The current of emigration from this state has swelled to a torrent," wrote Pease and Niles in their Connecticut gazeteer of 1819. From Maine alone ten to fifteen thousand are thought to have removed between 1810 and 1820. From Vermont, where in some townships actual want and suffering were a consequence of 1816's frigid weather, many families headed for western New York and Ohio. It was long before the influence of the disastrous years 1815 and 1816 were erased.[21]

The Mountain folks may have wondered about the cause of the bizarre weather. Like the epidemic, it was an affliction of biblical proportions. They could not have known that a mountain on the other side of the world affected them so.

In the past 10,000 years only one other volcano has exploded with that kind of gargantuan violence [as Thera in the Aegean in 1645 B.C.]: Tambora, in Indonesia, in 1816. It produced an ash cloud in the upper atmosphere that reflected sunlight back into space and produced the year without a summer. The cold led to ruinous harvests, hunger and even famine in the U.S., Europe and Russia.[22]

Families without a surplus or without a cash income must have suffered the most from the total loss of a year's crop. Perhaps the Mountain people helped each other. By 1810, most of them were related by marriage. But there was not enough good land to support another generation anyway. The west lured them away.

By 1810, several of Martin and Rebecca Preston's children had moved off the Mountain. Timothy, the eldest moved to Poughkeepsie and, in 1819, to the town of Washington. Elizabeth Kennedy moved to Onondaga County. Obadiah lived in Chatham in Columbia County. David, Philip, John, Eunice Hubbell, and Abigail Wolcott remained on the Mountain. A grandson named Allen Kennedy probably lived with the childless David and Margery Preston.

Martin was seventy years old. He owned a square mile of land. He had his land surveyed sometime after 1816 and divided it into roughly equal size parcels for each of his children. Philip died in 1816, leaving Annis, his widow, and his son, eighteen-year-old Clark. Martin marked one of the parcels for Clark in place of his father. Although Timothy, Obadiah, and Elizabeth had moved away, Martin set aside a parcel for each of them.[23]

In addition to the Philleo and Rust farms, Martin had acquired Simeon Cummins' farm. His grandson Ebenezer Preston II, son of John, would own the farm that had been Valentine Wheeler's. David Preston owned the large farm just south of his father's. When David died, he left it to his nephews Allen and David Kennedy. David also left land to another nephew, Thomas J. Wolcott.[24]

Across the state line, Martin's nephew Ebenezer Preston Jr. still owned most of the six hundred acres of the Schagticoke lands he had purchased in 1801. When he died in 1813, his many children inherited the Mountain land.

Around 1820, Martin Preston set aside an acre of his land for a public school. This land was across the road from Simeon Cummins' old house at the intersection still known as "Schoolhouse Corner." The Mountain was set off as one of Dover's rural school districts, known as "the Mountain District." Teachers lived with local families during the school year, alternating from one farm to another every few weeks. After a time, literacy arrived. Deeds marked by an "x" became less common. In time, some of the Mountain children grew up to be teachers themselves. But in the entire history of Preston Mountain, the only communal institutions, save one, were the school and the cemetery, both provided by Martin Preston. The other was a house and lot called the "charity lands," where one or two impoverished men lived from time to time, supported by a "poor tax" in Dover. The location of the charity lands is unknown, as the deed fails to identify the site.[25]

Over in Kent, Abraham Fuller died in 1807. In 1802, Abraham and Ozias Buell deeded one hundred acres along the New York line to Stephen Chase of Schodak, New York, "excepting and reserving to ourselves what mining minerals we own on said land."[26] These one hundred acres lay just north of Ebenezer Preston's six hundred acres (obtained from the Schagticokes), and just east of the Dunbar, Hill, and Jackson farms in New York. The Fuller/Buell deed and mortgage are the earliest evidence that iron people might be interested in Preston Mountain. It also suggests a reason why Ebenezer and other valley business people coveted the Mountain land.

Chapter Eleven
Iron, Wood, and Land

The iron industry overwhelmed northwest Connecticut and adjacent New York in the nineteenth century. It is difficult today to imagine conditions as they must have been in 1830. Today, forests surround us. We breathe clean air, and we see stars and sunlight without a filter of smoke. We cannot conceive of how different an environment existed in 1830. Forges and furnaces ringed Preston Mountain. The Housatonic River watershed, from Bull's Bridge north to Massachusetts, including all the adjacent towns in New York, constituted the most heavily industrialized region of the new United States. William Trapp Hopson, scion of one of Kent's iron families, described it: "Charcoal iron made in the Housatonic Valley was the main source of the iron supply of the country for pig iron, wrought iron and steel up to about 1840 and there were at on time twenty-seven furnaces in operation in this section."[1]

What had been a kind of cottage industry of small forges became, in 1826, something much larger. In that year, all three of the Kent furnaces started up. Macedonia, Bull's Bridge, and Kent furnaces all "went into blast." The furnaces produced much more iron than the forges. They also required far more charcoal to fuel them. Edward M. Kirby writes in *Echoes of Iron*: "a total of about 600 acres of forest was required to make the necessary amount of charcoal for a blast furnace for one year." In Kent alone, three furnaces consumed 1,800 acres of forest a year, 18,000 acres in ten years, and 36,000 acres in twenty years. Because it took at least twenty years for a cut forest to regenerate sufficiently to be cut again for charcoal, the three Kent furnaces required more forest than existed in the entire town of Kent, which amounted to about 30,000 acres. Preston Mountain became a critical source of charcoal for the Kent furnaces.[2]

Since virtually every home was heated with wood and was constructed of wood, it is inescapable that the entire region was denuded of trees during the first half of the nineteenth century. The soft outlines of forested hills became harsh, rocky spines looming over the valleys like the Scottish Highlands. Without trees and their root structures, the Mountain soil could not hold water. In each storm and freshet, water raced off the uplands, carving V-shaped gullies in the Mountain flanks and turning roads into streambeds. The fertile soil was carried into the valleys.

But the iron industry caused a more immediate impact on the environment—smoke. The furnaces produced great volumes of smoke. At the same time, the hills were dotted with stacks of wood being burned for charcoal. Each stack burned for about a month until the wood was properly charred. When the wind blew from the south, the smoke from Kent and Preston Mountain drifted north over Sharon. When the wind blew from the north, the smoke from Salisbury wafted down over the Housatonic Valley. People could not escape the smoke.

Though the iron industry changed people's lives in many bad ways, it also provided jobs. Teamster hauled ore, lime, and charcoal to the furnaces, and they hauled iron from the furnaces to schooners on the Hudson at Poughkeepsie. The Bull's Bridge furnace used ore hauled from the Fenn ore pit on Quaker Hill. Kent furnace and Macedonia used ore from the Kent ore bed southeast of the village. Slow-moving teams of oxen moved it along the rutted roads.

At the furnaces, masons constructed the stone stacks and carpenters hammered together the huge structures on top of the stacks. There were a variety of menial jobs, many of them filled with boys, some as young as ten. The iron master supervised all the work.

Increasingly, as the nineteenth century passed, heads of family on the Mountain were classified in the census records as "colliers" or "laborers" instead of "farmers." The colliers cut the timber, stacked it, and burned it for charcoal. Often, they also worked as teamsters to haul the charcoal to the furnaces. Some of these men worked at charcoal-making on their own farms, treating it as a "cash crop." Others worked for wages or "piece-work" on land iron companies or their owners owned.

The colliers worked everywhere in northwest Connecticut and eastern Dutchess County. Even today, the signs of their presence are ubiquitous in the hills. The forest that is now Macedonia Park supplied the furnace near Fuller Mountain Road. The hills around the park are dotted with leveled circles, thirty feet or so in diameter—charcoal "bottoms" or "pits." Some of these circles were built into steep hillsides with stone retaining walls to hold them there.

Preston Mountain is also covered with charcoal pits, most of them on the steep, rocky hills. But the farm woodlots were also cut and burned; charcoal was too valuable to leave any forest standing. Trees were felled, bucked into four-foot lengths, and these billets were stacked vertically on the leveled circles, all leaning inward toward the center. Once two and three levels had been stacked, the pile formed a dome shape, like a haystack. Colliers covered the stack with sod and wet leaves to reduce the amount of oxygen reaching the wood. Finally, inserting a lighted taper into the central base fired the stack. The collier controlled the burning by adjusting the amount of air flowing into the stack. It required constant vigilance. A stack with too much air flowing into it would blaze up and be consumed. Too little air would starve and extinguish the fire. Knowing the difference was an art.

It took weeks to burn a charcoal stack completely. Often the colliers and woodcutters built huts to live in near the stacks. Since the charcoal bottoms were used repeatedly, the huts, too, saw repeated use. Their builders constructed them carefully, with fine stone hearths or fireplaces for cooking and heating. Today, several such fireplaces stand free on Preston Mountain, the wood huts they once heated having rotted into the earth around them.

Once the burning was finished, the charcoal had to cool before it could be transported. Overseeing this process also required know-how. Kirby writes:

> When. . .the charcoal had cooled, it was transported to the furnace area in crib-shaped wagons and stored in large sheds. The charcoal cooling stage was a very important part of the total process. If the burning was not complete, exposure to the open air would result in

the ignition and burning of the charcoal. One more than one occasion after leaving the load for the night, a hapless teamster returned the next day to find only a heap of ashes and the few metal remains of his wagon.[3]

Oxen drew the charcoal wagons up the mountains to the burned stack where the product was loaded. It was a tedious and dirty job. The blackened billets had to be preserved as whole as possible—not broken up for shoveling. According to William Trapp Hopson, "Great care was taken in handling charcoal to prevent undue breakage, small pieces would be worthless." Such work required close contact between the men and the charcoal. As a result, the workers were black from head to foot. Hopson wrote that the colliers were "nearly all foreigners," implying that the work was too dirty, too rugged, or too dangerous for Yankees. Preston Mountain farmers must have been an exception. Hopson reported:[4]

> A few natives made charcoal on their own land and delivered it at the furnace. These colliers constructed log cabins to live in "while on the job" and they lived principally on salt pork, beans and potatoes. . . ."[5]

Colliers on Preston Mountain developed a peculiar reputation.

> Mt. Algo and the Dover Mountain was especially infested with rattlesnakes so that "medicine" had to be kept on hand with the natural result that snake bites were frequently anticipated by several days. On the whole, however, these men and their crews were competent and reliable and eventually made good citizens.[6]

Their work was dirty, lonely, and dangerous, but the colliers seemed to find some enjoyment in it. Of necessity, they were resourceful and self-reliant people. A mistake could be costly; there were no emergency services, fire departments, tow trucks, ambulances, or the like. Miles Waldron, a man who worked in the iron industry in Kent, remembered Martin Preston's great-grandson, Allen P. Kennedy.

> Allen Kennedy, he said, had a farm over near Dover Mountain. I never knew him to leave a load of charcoal standing in the wagon and his wagons never broke down with a load. Whenever he would notice that an axle or any important part was worn he at once made

a new one and thus avoided a breakdown and loss of a day or two in repairing the damage. He succeeded because he did not believe in taking chances.[7]

The Allen P. Kennedy house, probably built by David Preston in the 1700s.

The 1820s witnessed the beginning of a trend—the conveyance of land on Preston Mountain to iron companies or to men who were in the iron business. Some of the land may have been acquired for its potential to produce iron ore. More likely, the charcoal-hungry furnaces built in 1826 sharply increased the demand for woodland.

On the Kent portion of the Mountain, the following deeds were recorded:

In 1826, Abijah Preston sold 141 acres to Alpheus Fuller and Nathaniel Perry, who, in turn sold it to the Kent Iron Mfg. Company. This parcel was part of the 600 acres acquired by Ebenezer Preston, Jr. from the Schagticokes. Abijah was Ebenezer's son.[8]

In 1827, Ebenezer Preston [son of Ebenezer, Jr.] sold 52 acres of the former Schagticoke land to the Ousatonic Iron Mfg. Company.[9]

In 1830, John Preston the II conveyed Abel Rust's sawmill to Timothy and Dwight Chamberlain. This land bordered a parcel owned by Levi Stone, one of the principals in the Macedonia furnace operation.[10]

In 1831, Hagar Chapel and her children sold 87 acres to Rufus Fuller, who ran the Macedonia furnace. This land was also part of the 600 acres Ebenezer Preston, Jr. had acquired from the Schagticokes.[11]

In 1868, Obed Wing, Ebenezer Preston's grandson, sold 183 acres to the Kent Iron Company.[12]

In Dover, the following parcels passed to iron interests:

In 1825, John and Huldah Booth conveyed 29 acres to Lewis Lockwood of Sharon and John Williams of Salisbury. Williams was in the iron business through contracts with the Kent Iron Works. This land lay immediately to the west of Prince Dunbar's farm.[13]

In 1828, John and Lois Myrick sold 25 acres to Linus Winegar. The parcel was on the State line between Michael Jackson's farm and John Preston II.[14]

In 1834, Hagar Chapel and her children sold their homestead farm of 67 acres to Rufus Fuller.[15]

In 1832, Jacob Green sold 25 acres of the old John Bolt farm to the Ousatonic Iron Mfg. Company.[16]

In 1834, Timothy Preston [Martin's son] sold 51 acres to the Ousatonic Iron Company; The parcel was described in the deed as "a lot formerly in possession of William Bradshaw and called Bradshaw lands." The old Tory's farm became a charcoal woodlot. That same year, Timothy sold 42 ? acres he had acquired from his father adjacent to the Bradshaw parcel to the same iron company.[17]

In 1863, Abijah Preston sold a large parcel to Stuart Hopson & Co.[18]

Over seven hundred acres passed in these deeds, and there were probably more such transfers. It represented a large shift of ownership from resident farmers or homesteaders to nonresident owners. The land had become a kind of commodity.

Some changes of ownership in this period were involuntary. The rise of the iron interests on Preston Mountain coincided with the falling fortunes of the poor on Preston Mountain, particularly the poor African Americans.

By 1820, the first generation African American settlers were either very elderly or dead. London Hill probably died in 1804; Prince Dunbar died in 1813; Aaron Chapel survived until 1832 when he died at age eighty-two. They all left their farms to widows and children by virtue of intestacy (none of them had a will). These farms probably could no longer support the large number of people who depended on them. The African American people went into debt to tradesmen and to their neighbors, and, ultimately, lost their homes.

In March 1826, Prince Dunbar's son Robert possessed his father's place. He became indebted to Dover storekeeper John M. Tabor in the amount of $56.16. Tabor's store was in Dover Plains, at the intersection of the lane to the Stone Church and what is now Route 22. Tabor obtained a judgment against Robert and arranged to have John A. Wood, sheriff of Dutchess County, execute on the judgment by selling the Dunbar farm at auction sale. The purchaser was John M. Tabor himself. He paid $74.00 for the place. The deed into Tabor described the farm as: "Bounded on the north by Michael Jackson; on the west by John Williams [the iron man] and George Hoofcoot and Aaron Chapple' and on the east by Aaron Chapple and the Connecticut line, Containing 100 acres more or less."[19]

Thus, the Dunbar property had grown by forty acres in the quarter century since Prince bought it from Nathan Soule. But it diminished in value from $95.00 to $74.00, a reduction from $1.58 per acre to $.74 per acre. The auction sale may not have brought the full market value of the property, but it seems strange that, given the obvious demand for Mountain woodland, the land values had fallen by half in twenty-five years.

George Hoofcoot, the adjoining landowner, was a lawyer. His sister Betsy had married Nathan Soule's son, Thomas. George and Hannah owned a farm near the Dunbar and Hill farms. In 1820, London Hill had been dead for sixteen years (assuming he died in 1804, which is not certain). His widow, Grace, and his many children owned the farm as a matter of interstate law, though no estate had yet been filed for London. In 1819, George Hoofcoot filed a petition in the Dutchess County Surrogate Court, stating that when London Hill died interstate in 1804, he owed money to several creditors: forty dollars to Bradley Mills; fifteen dollars to Aaron Chapel; and ninety-five dollars to George Hoofcoot himself. Hoofcoot asked the court to name him the administrator of the estate for the purpose of paying the creditors.[20]

The court's file contains no explanation for why it took fifteen years after London's death to file an estate, nor does it set forth the nature of his debts. On October 13, 1819, the Dutchess County Surrogate Court appointed George Hoofcoot administrator. London's heirs were notified of the proceedings when they were served 'citations.' Those included were Grace Hill, Ruth Dunbar, Aaron and Hagar Chapel, Joseph, Richard, and Caleb Hill, and Queen Chapel (married to Aaron Chapel Jr.). None of London's heirs appeared in court to contest the claims.

In 1820, the court ordered the sale of the Hill farm to satisfy the creditors. Notices were posted at John Preston's tavern, the store of Uriah Gregory and John M. Tabor, and at the dwelling house of London Hill. The notice of sale described the farm as consisting of one hundred acres. The sale was advertised to take place at the store of Uriah Gregory and John M. Tabor on Saturday, August 26, 1820, "between the hours of ten o'clock in the forenoon and four o'clock in the afternoon of said day. . . ."

George Hoofcoot filed the report of the sale with the court two years later, on May 4, 1822. The sale took place as scheduled, and "a number of persons attended the sale and a number of bids made. . . ." The high bidder was Robert Benson, who paid $110.00 for the farm. No deed for London Hill's farm was ever recorded in Dutchess County for Robert Benson or anyone else. When George Hoofcoot died in 1853, his sons owned the Hill and Dunbar farms and other lands, totaling, in all, over three hundred acres.

His neighbors on the Mountain hired George Hoofcoot to be their lawyer. Many, including David Preston, named him administrator or executor of their estates. He had apparently earned their trust and respect. It is unfortunate that he did not set forth the nature of London Hill's debts in the application to the Dutchess County Surrogate Court. However, given that Aaron Chapel was related to Hill by marriage, it is doubtful that Chapel would have joined in the lawyer's application if he thought it unjust.

Aaron Chapel died in 1831 and was buried alongside his daughter Lucy in the cemetery on Martin Preston's farm. Aaron presents a bit of a mystery. Though there were white Chapels living in Kent and

Sharon in the eighteenth century, there is no evidence that they owned slaves. Where did Aaron come from? Was he a freed slave? How did he come to settle on Preston Mountain? What is known is that he was married at least twice: first, to Martha Obadiah in Amenia in 1776 and, later, to Hagar. He lived long enough on the Mountain to establish a substantial farm. Ebenezer Preston Jr. trusted him enough to hold his mortgage. His fellow townspeople had enough confidence in him to elect him overseer of highways at the first Dover town meeting in 1807. There is every indication that Aaron Chapel commanded and received respect.[21]

We know almost nothing about Michael Jackson. Adjoining deeds place his homestead along the state line between Prince Dunbar and John Preston II (there was a Winegar woodlot between Jackson and Preston). There is no record of his purchasing or selling his farm. We do not know the names of his wife or children. He appeared in the federal census of 1810 and 1820. He was gone by 1830.[22]

By 1835, "all other free people" had either sold or lost their homes on Preston Mountain, and their families were dispersed. Like the emigrants who moved to Russia, New York, these families were not replaced. Large landholdings replaced small homesteads, and many of the new owners were absentee owners. The use of the land changed as well. Charcoal became the premiere crop. Soon, the first generation of settlers would be gone.

Chapter Twelve
"Out of the Smoke of Their Chimneys"

MARTIN PRESTON DIED ON FEBRUARY 23, 1833, at age nine-ty-two . Rebecca had died in 1824. They lie side-by-side in the burying ground on the hill south of their home.

Martin left no will. In March 1833, his son John, together with two other men, John Jewitt and John Wing, filed a petition for letters of administration of Martin's personal estate. Only five children survived the old man: Timothy, David, Obadiah, John, and Elizabeth Kennedy. The estate file lists thirteen grandchildren. Martin's son David, and three grandsons, Clark Preston, Thomas J. Wolcott, and Allen Kennedy, still farmed on the Mountain.[1]

At his death, Martin held promissory notes from twenty-one people—more than fifteen hundred dollars in loans. Some of the notes were classified as "desperate" or "very desperate," meaning, presumably, that the debtors were unlikely to pay them. The largest such note was from a grandson, Martin Preston II for$302.48. Daughters Anna Fairchild and Elizabeth Kennedy had borrowed from him, as had his sons Obadiah and John.

In the year following his death, Martin's children hastened to sell off his land. Elizabeth Kennedy sold the house and sixty acres to Darius Sherman. Timothy sold the land on the Connecticut border to the Ousatonic Iron Company. Clark Preston and Thomas J. Wolcott acquired some of their grandfather's lands from their aunts and uncles. Thomas J. Wolcott left the Mountain for several years, but moved back by 1850.[2]

Martin's estate was probably quite large for the era. He owned over a square mile of land. At a time when farms sold for a few hun-

Martin Preston's grave. Rebecca Preston's stone has fallen over.

dred dollars, the fifteen hundred dollars in notes that Martin held qualified him as a significant lender. Given the "desperate" classification of the notes, he was probably generous, but not prudent. Perhaps the inventory of personal property Martin owned, which was filed with his estate, was a truer measure of his life and wealth.

Inventory of Personal Property
Estate of Martin Preston

Specie on hand	$93.26	Bill on Chemical Bank	$2.00
Bill on Fairfield County Bank	$2.00	14 quilts	$21.00
7 old woolen sheets	$14.00	3 beds with bowlsters	$21.00
3 straw ticks	$1.50	32 linnen sheets	$16.00
1 carpit $3.00		15 towels	$3.75
5 table cloths	$3.00	2 cheese cloths	$0.50
1 pair of trowsers not made	$1.50	2 ? yards fulled cloth	$2.50
wearing apparel	$25.00	16 pieces of pewter	$3.00
16 spoons – pewter	$0.25	1 lot of earthen ware	$0.50
knives and forks	$0.50	1 lot tin ware	$3.00
2 tables and stand	$0.50	2 brass kittles	$4.00
1 hatchet	$1.50	1 case and 10 bottles	$2.00
13 chairs	$1.62	1 warming pan	$1.00
5 iron pots and kettles	$4.00	1 pair andirons with tongs	$1.50
1 frying pan	$0.50	3 trammels, 1 gridiron	$1.62
2 pair of steel yards	$1.00	1 dresser and 4 chests	$3.00
1 clock and case	$3.00	6 bowls and 2 chums	$1.25
2 candle sticks and		5 earthen pots and 2 jugs	$0.87
1 chopping knife	$0.25		
3 old cupboards	$1.25	1 (?) and 2 hand saws	$3.00
1 lot of scythe sticks	$10.00	2 hoes	$0.50
blacksmith tools	$5.00	1 pair of horse shakels	$0.50
5 old adzes	$1.25	2 ploughs	$1.50
1 spinning wheel, 2 grain cradles, 1 shovel and 1 spade			$2.25
1 old harness	$5.00	13 lbs. of leather	$3.62
1 crow bar	$1.00	5 wheels	$0.25
1 pair old portmanteaus	$0.25	1 sett shoe maker's tools	$1.00
2 old saddles and 2 bridles	$1.00	3 ox yokes, staples and rings	$2.25
2 ox chains	$2.00	1 axe	$0.50
1 waggon, old	$7.00	1 old cart	$3.00
1 harrow	$2.00	1 grind stone and crank	$1.00
1 ox sled	$0.50	1 bush hook and bog hoe	$0.25
1 hive of bees	$1.50	2 iron wedges	$0.25

4 barrels of cider and barrels	$8.00	14 old cider barrels	$1.25
4 kegs	$0.50	1 cheese press	$1.50
3 meat casks and meat	$45.00	1 heap of potatoes	$3.00
barrels of soap	$4.50	1 crib of corn	$10.00
18 bushels of rye	$13.75	10 bushels of oats	$12.50
4 bushels of buckwheat	$1.50	1 looking glass	$0.25
5 tubs and 2 wooden pails	$1.00	1 French gun and equipage	$5.00
1 fowling piece	$2.25	4 empty bags 2 rye flour	$5.00
3 bushels of salt	$2.25	? wire sieve	$0.50
5 drawing knives	$1.00	2 wheel heads	$0.50
1 small spinning wheel	$1.00	1 ? bushels beans and peas	$1.00
18 lbs. of flax	$1.62	4 old reeds and reed box	$1.00
1 corn basket and riddle	$0.37	2 runs of yarn	$0.25
1 bellows and 2 hammers	$0.37	1 lot of old books	$0.37
1 pair 8-year-old oxen	$75.00	1 pair 6-year-old oxen	$60.00
1 3-year-old farrow heifer	$12.00	1 farrow cow	$13.00
1 bay mare	$50.00	7 cows with calf	$122.502
2-year-old steers and 3 2-year-old heifers			$45.00
4 yearlings	$20.00	1 colt	$10.00
4 swine	$16.00	9 old sheep, 2 lambs, bell	$20.00
14 dung hill fowls	$2.62	9 lbs. of honey	$1.12
10 lbs. sugar	$0.75	3 lbs. 14 oz. beeswax	$0.97
9 lbs tallow	$0.90	7 lbs. candles	$0.70
4 cheeses weighing 47 lbs.	$2.82	3 hams	$3.60
2 wooden bottles	$0.25	1 slate	$0.12
1 lot of vials and 3 glasses	$0.25	1 cider mill and press	$2.50
1 mouse trap	$0.25	1 lot of loose rounds	$1.00

4 powder horns, canister and powder, bullett mould, shot mould, spoon mould, 2 shot bags & shot razor, strap and box, 3 old sheep shears, 1 dozen gun flints, 1 dog chain and strap, old cards, candle wicks, nails, vest knitting pins, bottles and spirit turpentine, pine boards, old baskets, brush, pins, knife, spectacles, bells, trowels, buckets, tar bucket and tar, old tub & jug jointers, hog troughs – appraised at – $2.00

This, plus potatoes in the hole at $15.00, grain on the ground at $13.50, and hay at $23.00, constituted Martin Preston's wealth. He owned tools, utensils, livestock, and the products of his labor; useful things, all of them, but no luxuries save "1 lot of old books." Presumably, owning the books meant that someone in the household could read. It was not Martin; he signed his name with an "x."[3]

Eighteen head of cattle, four swine, and nine sheep constitute a small farm by today's standards. But the feed for these animals was sewn, harvested, and moved entirely by hand labor. The oldest brace of oxen were only eight years old, meaning that they were trained to the yoke when Martin was in his eighties. Maybe he engaged a hired man or two in his last years. The work of his farm would seem too much for a ninety-year-old man. His sons and grandsons ran their own farms. The inventory makes it clear that he stayed on his own place. He did not move in with a son and merge their stock. He was a rugged old man, no doubt, perhaps a lonely man. There is a hint of Rebecca's loss in the item, "one pair of trowsers not made."

For almost seventy years, Martin and Rebecca had worked to create a farmstead for themselves and their issue on the Mountain. They intended that it would be their family home for generations to come. Miles of stone walls attest to their quest for permanence. There was nothing unique in this endeavor; the pioneers of every American frontier stopped when they had reached their promised land and then built for the future. But the American spirit had changed by 1834—each generation now looked for a new frontier. Young people had the urge to move on. Even if the Mountain had consisted of deep, fertile cropland, there would not have been enough of it for the large families. The westward movement would probably have taken most of the younger generation.

Though more of them left the Mountain than stayed, it seemed that Martin's children and grandchildren revered the old man. One measure of their regard for him may be reckoned from his many namesakes. Thomas and Abigail Wolcott had Martin Wolcott; Allen P. and Francis Kennedy had Martin Kennedy; Timothy and Rachel Preston had Martin Preston II; Obadiah and Amy Preston had Judd Martin Preston, honoring both parents.

A further measure of Martin's legacy to the Mountain community was recorded in deeds after his passing. In 1833, his children and grandchildren joined in conveying the old Simeon Cummins farm to Martin's grandson Clark Preston. At the conclusion of the description of the land, the deed recited: "school house and lot now fenced off not included." The schoolhouse was built in a vale at the west side of an intersection of roads still known as "Schoolhouse Corners." Recent logging has destroyed any evidence of the school's existence, but the schoolhouse lot is a green meadow in the forest. No records of the school's early years survive except the reality of Mountain children growing up to be teachers, doctors, and ministers.[4]

In 1836, Martin's grandson sold some of Martin's former land. The deed stated, "Excepting and reserving a right of passing [to the cemetery] to the use of the public forever and passing to it at all times from the road by way of the bars first east of the burial ground." The burial ground was not located in some unwanted corner of Martin's farm, nor was it preserved for the private use of the Preston family. It lies away from the road in the middle of the best piece of farmland on the place—and it was available to all.[5]

While the Prestons were dispersing, new settlers were arriving on the Mountain. One of the promissory notes that Martin Preston held was from Abijah Patchin and his brother Eli Patchin, for twenty-one dollars. It was marked "desperate." These men were newcomers to Preston Mountain. Perhaps no Mountain family more clearly illustrated the westering spirit than the Patchins.[6]

Abijah and Eli were probably the sons of an impoverished veteran of the Revolution, Elijah Patchin. Elijah was a weaver from Stamford, Connecticut. He served from 1775 until the end of the war and was discharged as a corporal. According to the Stamford history, by 1820, Elijah "owns no home or land or personal estate…."[7]

His sons fared little better. Abijah was born in 1789. According to his great-grandson, Carl Henry Patchin, "Abijah Patchin as a young man lived in the Town of Dover and worked as a carpenter. Sometime before 1813 he moved to Preston Mountain where his first wife died in that year." Abijah's first wife was Lydia Roberts, daughter of Daniel Roberts. Lydia died on May 18, 1813, probably in the epidemic of that year. They had two children, Rachel and Daniel, born, respectively, in 1810 and 1812. Abijah was thus left a widower with two toddlers to care for. He quickly married again, to Huldah Bolt, daughter of Mountain farmer John Bolt. Their son Mark Abijah was born on April 7, 1814, less than eleven months after the death of Lydia. More children followed quickly: Hiram, David, Levi Gould, Mary Jane, and Henry. When Huldah died in 1844, Abijah remarried again, this time to Rebecca Kennedy, widow of Martin Preston's grandson, Allen Kennedy.[8]

The practice of prompt remarriage after the death of a spouse recurs often in the Preston Mountain history. Today, the custom is to "wait a decent interval," a mourning period, between such marriages. Assuming that their son Mark Abijah was a full-term baby, Abijah married Huldah about a month after his first wife died. Marriage was a necessity. Abijah had neither the skills nor the time to cook, mind the babies, sew, or perform the hundreds of functions a nineteenth century woman accomplished daily. Huldah could not plow, fell timber or build walls. A man's work in 1813 required brute strength. Even if they had no emotional or sexual attraction to one another, in a very real sense, they needed each other.

Apparently, Abijah and Huldah lived such an impoverished life on the Mountain that they could not afford to support their children. Mark stayed with someone in South Dover; Rachel lived at Wings' station; Hiram boarded at Dover; Kent and Warren boarded in Connecticut; Levi Gould "went further south," to Fairfield, Danbury, and New Jersey. "Levi Gould lived with a Quaker family, name unknown, who treated him as a son, and he received his education in Fairfield, Conn."[9]

Levi became a schoolteacher in Flagtown, New Jersey, where he met his bride, Catherine Gumble. In 1845, he emigrated to the western prairie in Hancock County, Illinois. Catherine followed later, traveling by boat down the Ohio River. During a severe storm, the boat's captain ordered all luggage thrown overboard to prevent swamping. Catherine lost her wedding dress and other treasures.[10]

They settled near Chili Center and Bowen, Illinois. There they bought three hundred and ten acres from the United States Government. Levi and Catherine lived in a log cabin, where the first five of their twelve children were born. Levi hauled his grain and livestock to market in Quincy, taking two days to make the eighty-mile round trip. Their daughter, Lillian, wrote a memoir of their pioneering life:

> He and Mother made all the improvements and they soon had a very fertile and beautiful farm with many trees and house and barns and stock, with a wonderful orchard of all kinds of fruit. He gave a corner of the farm for a log schoolhouse to be built. . . . The Methodist Quarterly meetings were sometimes held in Father's locust grove and Mother prepared dinner for those who came without food, often

feeding as many as forty people. Mother spun the yarn, knit the stockings and mittens for her husband and twelve children, made coats, pants and overcoats for Father and the boys, and all other clothes while the children were growing up, often setting up until after midnight after her days' work was done to do her sewing, all by hand until 1860 when she bought a sewing machine.[11]

Despite the large and beautiful farm that she described, it seemed that none of the twelve children stayed to farm it. They moved on west, to Missouri, Colorado and Arizona; all except Lillian—she moved back to New Jersey.

Hancock County, Illinois, was a dangerous place in 1845. Nauvoo, the Mormon capital, was in Hancock County. Joseph Smith, founder of the Church of Jesus Christ of Latter Day Saints, and his brother were murdered in the Hancock county jail in Carthage in 1845, barely twelve miles from the Patchin homestead. Mobs soon attacked the Mormons at Nauvoo, destroying the temple, and compelling the saints to flee westward. Still, Levi felt he had found the promised land. On July 21, 1845, he wrote his brother Hiram:

> Respected brother:
> I received a letter from you this morning, stating that you were going to start for Illinois on the first of Sept. Glad to hear that there is courage enough in one more of the Patchins to get out of the smoke of their chimneys, and I wish to add to persevere. I have just come in from the harvest field, and am all dripping with sweat and have seized the pen to try to give you an answer for your short epistle.[12]

Hiram did move west, married Susan Powell in Hancock County, and moved on to Butler, Missouri. He and his wife both died as the result of injuries suffered when a "cyclone turned over his house" in 1880. The several letters that Levi sent Hiram never mention their parents back on Preston Mountain. Maybe there was a bit of contempt for Patchins who had neither the courage nor the perseverance to get out of the smoke of their chimneys.[13]

Abijah Patchin died of cancer in 1862. In 1863, Levi and Hiram's older brother, Mark Abijah, sued them to partition their parents' property on the Mountain. The referee auctioned off the place on November 12, 1863. The estranged siblings must have shared the proceeds.[14]

Abijah's last wife, Rebecca Kennedy Patchin, moved to a house on a small patch of ground near the old James Agard place. It was shown in the 1867 Beers atlas map as the "Widow Patchin" place. Three of her children by her first husband, Allen Kennedy, married three children of Eli Patchin, her second husband's brother: Allen P. Kennedy married Frances Patchin; David L. Kennedy married Irene Patchin; Sarah Kennedy married Edwin C. Patchin. Allen P. and Frances Kennedy became the parents of Erben Kennedy, the last of the original community.

Martins' son, David Preston, died in 1846. He left a will naming the lawyer George Hufcut (Hoofcoot) as his executor. David left no children. Though his wife Margery survived him, he left his farm and other land to various great-nephews and nieces. Thomas Wolcott (acquired a meadow and an old field known as the "Draper Lot." Eliza and Maria Kennedy acquired a small parcel south of James Agard's garden, probably where the widow Rebecca Kennedy Patchin lived. The rest of David's large farm went to the brothers, Allen P. Kennedy and David L. Kennedy, "to be divided equally between them when David becomes twenty-one."[15]

There were still several descendants of Martin and Rebecca farming on the Mountain: Clark Preston, David and Allen Kennedy, and Thomas Wolcott. A few years later, Thomas' son William Wolcott owned the largest farm on the Mountain—the old Luke Wolcott place south of Wolf Swamp.

There were new families at most of the other old farms. The Shermans owned much of Martin Preston's place; the Patchins worked John Bolt's homestead. People named Wheeler, Dingee, Cook, Orton, and Griffin were their neighbors. But much of the land that had first been settled in the eighteenth century was allowed to grow back to brush and woods. Valley farmers purchased some places for winter woodlots. Iron companies used more of it for charcoal.

By 1850, when the Harlem Division of the New York Central Railroad reached Dover Plains, Preston Mountain was no longer a desirable address. The railroad made farming in the valley profitable; milk, fruit, and livestock could easily be marketed in New York City. Farms near the railheads at Wingdale, Dover Furnace, and Dover Plains grew larger and richer. The Mountain farms could not compete. But there was one group of people who still gravitated to the Mountain—the poor.

There existed no national or statewide welfare system in the nineteenth century. Communities were legally responsible for the paupers who lived there. . That is probably why the earliest Dover town records reflect several expenditures to men for escorting people to other towns; the local taxpayers tried to avoid supporting another town's poor. The responsibility was statutory. New York's 1788 law stated: "Every city and town shall support and maintain their own poor."[16]

In 1825, the overseers of the poor in Dover were Abijah Preston (Ebenezer Junior's son) and Jackson Wing. That year, the overseers took title to an acre and a quarter of Preston Mountain land from Jacob and Elizabeth Rider. The parcel conveyed to Wing and Preston was described in the deed as "the same place where Bradly Phileo now resides."[17]

In 1826, Abijah Preston and Reuben Chapman purchased 119 acres from Azariah Howland, beginning at the northwest corner of the "charitrie (charity) land." In 1838, Thomas J. Wolcott and his wife Jane sold four and a half acres nearby to Abijah Preston, describing the parcel as, "Beginning at a great round rock southwest of the old home place of Josiah Bradshaw and Bradley Phileo, deceased." The one and a quarter acre "charitrie land" was a poorhouse. Josiah Bradshaw and Bradley Phileo were its inhabitants. Josiah was probably related to William Bradshaw, the old Tory, but the nature of the relationship is uncertain. The Phileo family genealogy said of Bradley Phileo: "He seems to have been a poor boy and early put out to a farmer and received a very limited education." Bradley married Lucy Odell before 1815, but "he died with a cancer about 1835." The genealogy claimed they were both buried "at Preston M. cemetery, Dover, N.Y., but, no tombstone marks their resting place. . . ."[18]

In addition to the poorhouse occupants, there were four Revolutionary War pensioners living on the Mountain; Silas Curtis, John Johnson, Darius Cook, and Anna Jones, widow of Isaac Jones. Anna Jones probably lived with her son Levi, who moved to the Mountain about 1806. The exact location of the home or homes of these pensioners remains uncertain.

Isaac Jones was seventy-five years old in 1820. His pension application indicated that he was a day laborer, but, due to age and infirmity, he was not able to do much labor. He claimed property valued at less than twenty-five dollars. When he died in 1834, Anna inherited his pension.[19]

Silas Curtis served with the Connecticut Line of the Constitutional Army during the Revolution. He also served in the war of 1812. His pension was eight dollars per month. Silas stated: "I am by occupation a shoe maker & I have no property but my small pittance of tools before mentioned [worth $7.50]."[20]

Darius Cook's petition claimed, "real estate, I have none." He listed a handful of items of personal property, asserting, "I am a carpenter by trade but on account of age and infirmities am unable to work. . . ."[21]

The sad litany of these petitions is too repetitive to be accidental. Every pension petition of the soldiers from Preston Mountain recited the same language, in substance: "due to age and infirmities am unable to work." Perhaps they learned from their peers the formula for obtaining a pension. Still, no doubt, they told the truth. A carpenter, a shoemaker and a day laborer all past middle age and all landless, must have been impoverished. Their neighbors scarcely had the wherewithal to pay them for their work, if, indeed, they hired them. Without land or livelihood it is difficult to see what drew these folks to the Mountain. Except for Cook, they were listed sequentially in the 1840 census, indicating that they lived near each other, or, perhaps, together. Perhaps someone made a home for these impoverished veterans or they sought each other's company for support.

Over the first ninety years of occupation on the Mountain, the settlers contributed their share to America's military. Although the Prestons avoided entangling themselves, most Mountain families boasted a soldier or two. They may have enlisted in greater proportion to their numbers than men elsewhere. Their poverty did not diminish their patriotism. This tradition continued as the Civil War tore apart American society.

Chapter Thirteen
The Civil War: "Tis Noble Thus To Die"

BY 1860, AS WAR THREATENED, Preston Mountain's population had shrunk. The 1850 federal census counted twenty-one households there; the New York State census of 1865 found only fifteen. Among the latter were five families descended from Martin and Rebecca Preston, headed by Clark Preston, Patty Hufcut, Allan P. Kennedy, Philip Wolcott, and William Wolcott. Other descendants of early settlers were Henry Hufcut, Edwin C. Patchin, William Stow, and William Phillow.

Newcomers on the Mountain included the families of Hiram Wheeler (a distant relation of the Revolutionary War officer Valentine Wheeler) and James Dingee. Hiram married Sabrina Edmonds (who often misspelled her name "Serbenia"). Two of their sons Harmon and Harrison acquired a small farm from Sabrina's relatives Samuel and Caroline Edmonds, in 1851.

This tiny "farm of land," slightly more than thirty acres, lay in a hollow on a sharp bend of the road west of Kennedy Bridge Brook (Crane Pond today). The Edmonds' deed described the place as "being on the highway leading from Canada Bridge to the top of the mountain." The road ran west from the brook, through the farm, over the mountain, and down, steeply into the Harlem Valley at the Dover/Amenia town line.[1]

Harmon and Harrison began farming their own land at young ages, respectively twenty-one years and nineteen years. Their father, Hiram, was a laborer in Dover. He was the youngest son of John B. Wheeler. Hiram and Sabrina had four minor children at home, the youngest only four. Getting the two older boys out on their own must have eased the parents' finances.[2]

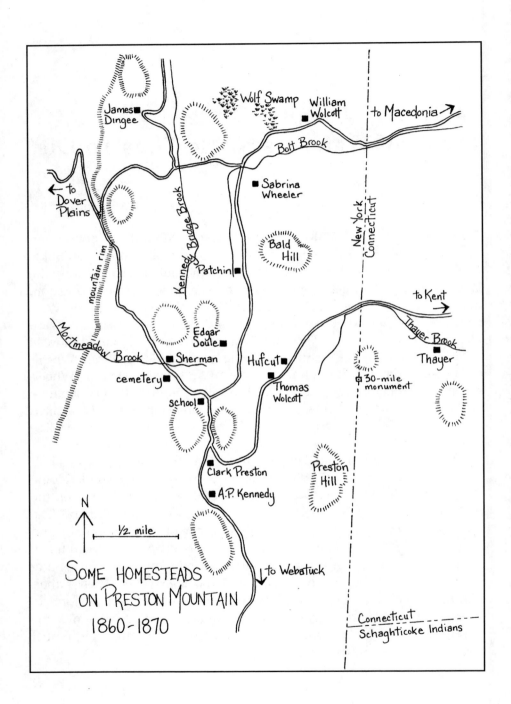

Wolf Swamp

William Wolcott

to Macedonia →

James Dingee

Bolt Brook

← to Dover Plains

Sabrina Wheeler

New York
Connecticut

Kennedy Bridge Brook

Bald Hill

Mountain rim

Patchin

to Kent →

Thayer Brook

Mortmeadow Brook

Edgar Soule

Thayer

Sherman

Hufcut

30-mile monument

cemetery

Thomas Wolcott

school

Preston Hill

Clark Preston

A.P. Kennedy

N

½ mile

SOME HOMESTEADS
ON PRESTON MOUNTAIN
1860-1870

↓ to Webatuck

Connecticut
Schaghticoke Indians

136

The young men probably worked at other trades to make ends meet; a thirty-acre mountain farm hardly provided a living. By 1860, their parents and brothers and sisters had also moved up on the Mountain. The 1867 Beers Atlas Map showed "H. Wheeler" occupying the farmland Valentine Wheeler had willed to his son John northwest of the "Bald Hill." The 1860 census showed that Harmon was back living with his parents. Harmon and Harrison conveyed their farm to their sister and brother-in-law Susan and Andrew Austin before 1862. On September 30, 1861, Harmon Wheeler enlisted as a private in Company 26, 6th Regiment of New York Cavalry. The Civil War came to Preston Mountain.[3]

Escape from Andersonville

FORT SUMTER, SOUTH CAROLINA, FELL ON APRIL 13, 1861. President Abraham Lincoln called on the northern states for 75,000 men to suppress the rebellion. New York's requisition called for about 14,000 men. Instead, the state produced about 30,000 soldiers. Americans went to war eagerly in 1861.[4]

Local communities competed to drum up support for the war. Prominent citizens conducted "war meetings" in several Dutchess County towns, trying to arouse patriotic fervor. One such meeting was held in Beekman on May 11, 1861. Dover's famous historian, Benson Lossing, addressed the crowd:

> Suddenly a thunder peal rolled over the land. It was the boom of the gun that hurled a rebel shot at Fort Sumter. It fell upon the dull ear of the North like the trumpet of the Archangel. Instantly the dead were raised. The millions of the loyal States, as one man, sprang to their feet and seized the weapons of war. Every heart was filled with courage and devotion. The life blood coursed swiftly through their veins. From every hill and valley a shout went up louder than ten thousand thunders. "The Union and the Government shall be preserved."[5]

Francis Atwater reported that over in Kent, "Enthusiasm ran wild."

> The firing on Fort Sumter awoke in the hearts of the people of Kent the slumbering military fire that had descended from the forefathers of 1776. It was the talk of the town, and a public meeting was called on April 29, 1861, for the purpose of taking into consideration the propriety of voting supplies to all who would volunteer into the service of the United States and go to the seat of war....[6]

How was a young man to resist such a spirit? Most soldiers of 1861 were old enough to have known some old soldiers of the Revolution—to have fallen under the spell of their war stories. Indeed, many of the 1861 generation had grandfathers and great-grandfathers who fought in the Revolution. This legacy, the warlike spirit, and colorful uniforms all exerted influence on the young men. The public would remain ignorant of the horrors of the war for many months.

In the beginning, the Civil War was an amateur affair. There were no standing armies and few professional soldiers on either side. Most career soldiers joined the Confederacy. In the north, counties formed volunteer regiments in which the smaller units, like companies, were comprised of men from one or two towns. This form of organization brought severe losses to some communities, while others suffered relatively few casualties. Kent, for example, lost many men in the final brutal campaigns in Virginia, at Petersburg and Cold Harbor. Meanwhile, most Dover soldiers served in General John Henry Ketcham's 150th Regiment, fighting in the south and in Sherman's march through Georgia to the sea. Dover's casualties, compared to Kent's, were light.[7]

Politics played a role in the appointment of officers at all levels. General Ketcham himself was a political choice, having never seen a battle when he took command of the 150th. James McPherson wrote, "These appointments made political sense but sometimes produced military calamity."

Finally, the soldiers themselves received virtually no training.

Civil War regiments learned on the battlefield to fight, not in the training camp. In keeping with the lack of professionalism, the training of recruits was superficial. It consisted mainly of the manual of arms [but little target practice], company and regimental drill in basic maneuvers, and sometimes brigade drill and skirmishing tactics.[8]

The young troops knew nothing of the complex art of moving an entire regiment or corps in battle. On July 21, 1861, the Union army faced its first big battle with the Confederates at Manassas, Virginia. By that afternoon, "the Northern army lost what little cohesion it had everywhere, as regiments continued to fight in a disconnected manner, stragglers began melting to the rear." The Union men succumbed to a spreading panic, discipline disappeared, and the battle was lost. It was by such hard experience that men learned to soldier.[9]

Martin and Rebecca Preston's great-grandson John Wolcott was born on the Mountain in 1825 to Thomas J. and Julia Wolcott. Luke Wolcott, the Revolutionary War militia officer was another of John's great-grandfathers. John Wolcott became a collier. His first wife, Sarah Lane of Kent, died in 1852. John moved west to Wyandotte, Michigan, to work in a foundry. He left his infant children with family in Kent. In 1862, he enlisted in Company D, 5th Regiment of the Michigan Cavalry. It was a three-year enlistment. In December, the 5th Michigan became part of the Michigan Cavalry Brigade, the "Michigan Wolverines," commanded by the flamboyant brigadier general George Armstrong Custer of Little Bighorn fame.[10]

The Wolverines distinguished themselves by being one of the first units engaged at Gettysburg. They were trying to prevent supplies and reinforcements from reaching Lee's army. After the battle, they harassed the retreating rebels all the way to the Potomac where they attacked the rear guard, killing 125 men and taking 1,500 prisoners.[11]

In 1864, the brigade fought a series of actions in Virginia, including battles in the Shenandoah Valley under General Phil Sheridan. During one of these confrontations, the southerners captured Private John Wolcott. By summer, he was a prisoner in the dreaded Confederate prison at Andersonville, Georgia. He was thirty-nine years old. Andersonville had become a synonym for inhumanity.

> A stockade camp of sixteen acres designed for 10,000 prisoners, Andersonville soon became overcrowded with captives from Sherman's army as well as from the eastern theatre. It was enlarged to twenty-six acres, in which 33,000 men were packed by August, 1864—an average of thirty-four square feet per man—without shade in a Deep South summer and with no shelter except what they could rig from sticks, tent flies, blankets and odd bits of cloth.... During some weeks in the summer of 1864 more than a hundred prisoners died every day in Andersonville. Altogether 13,000 of the 45,000 men imprisoned there died of disease, exposure or malnutrition.[12]

The US Government's website for Andersonville says that the site of the prison contains 13,737 graves.[13]

It is unclear how long John Wolcott endured these conditions. It could not have been for more than a few months because Andersonville contained no prisoners before February 1864. But John Wolcott did not die in Andersonville—he escaped.

At noon on August 7, 1864, Wolcott and Alfonso Barrows, a twenty-six-year-old soldier from the 1st Vermont Cavalry, headed for the swamps. Barrows later wrote an account of their escape. He began to plan to run off in July when he came down with chronic dysentery and realized he was becoming weaker. He looked for a partner to share the dangers. Barrows explains what happened one day as he was cutting wood outside the camp:[14]

> I heard a man say he wasn't going to stay very much longer. This was John Wolcott who belonged to the 7th Michigan Cavalry. We chopped wood together and when he said he would go with me I was sure that he meant it. . . . We planned to go in August, a week from the time John said we would go.[15]

Barrows and Wolcott hid a bag of provisions in the woods,

"eight dozen and ten biscuits and a small ham." They hired a soldier who had been a tailor to make two pairs of cotton trousers for them, "the same as those the Rebels wore." They learned from a teamster slave that Sherman's army confronted Atlanta, and that Atlanta was "a little northwest of Andersonville." It was actually more than a hundred miles. The slave also taught them that they could hide their scent from the bloodhounds by dousing their legs with a mixture of turpentine and onions. They soon found a better way.

Wolcott and Barrows ran into trouble from the start; they couldn't find where they had hidden the food. They persisted and finally found the sack. Barrows killed a skunk and removed its scent glands, which they carried in their pockets to confuse the dogs. That afternoon, they walked north through deep woods and cornfields until they encountered a temptation.

> When about two miles from the Stockade We went through a cornfield, which according to the southern custom had watermelons planted between the rows of corn. Bordering the cornfield was a canebrake swamp. We selected a nice melon from the patch, carried it into the canebrake, and sat down on a log for a feast. We had just commenced on it when we were startled by the baying of hounds. As they had a pack of eleven at the Stockade, naturally we thought they were on our track in spite of the free application of skunk essence. The melon was thrown aside and we started in a hurry for the brook and swamp which we intended to follow.[16]

But the hounds were not following them. It was a great relief to them. The rebels would have hanged them if they were caught; prisoners were allowed one mile from the camp, but it was death to venture farther than the mile.

Relief didn't last long, however. Three southern soldiers spotted them lying in the grass alongside a country road. But the soldiers turned out to be mere boys, eleven to fourteen years old. The boys demanded their passes. Trusting that the boys couldn't read, the escapees handed over their prison passes. The bluff worked. Barrows and Wolcott were free to move on.

They walked long into a dark, cloudy night, unsure that they were headed in the correct direction. It was too dark to read the compass. Finally, Barrows caught a lightning bug and they read their watch and compass by its glow; it was two o'clock in the morning and they were heading to Atlanta.

It began to rain the second day. The dampness soured their biscuits, but the two men were so hungry they ate them anyway. They began to encounter more people. The escapees' ragged appearance aroused suspicion. To avoid confrontations they took to the thickest brush and brambles, suffering cuts and scratches and torn clothing. While they were struggling through a thicket they heard a man calling to them.

> John Wolcott had the watch open. He snapped it shut. The man, not being able to see, thought the click thus made was a revolver. It frightened him and he ran off. We hurried on as fast as possible. On and on we went.[17]

They walked for many days and nights, swimming rivers and struggling through swamps. They both nearly drowned crossing a large river. Their food ran out. "A bone or two already thoroughly gnawed and what we could peel off in the way of dough that has stuck to the sides of the haversack was all there was." A widow gave them a little "hoe cake;" she told them "her husband, not wanting to go to war, had been taken out and killed by guerillas."[18]

Finally, after a bad night in a swamp full of "dead streams," they came to a big road. They walked down the road until almost dawn. "All at once, someone hollered: "Halt, who goes there?" It turned out there were three Union pickets hidden in the low pines at the side of the road."[19]

Wolcott and Barrows were safe. Back in northern lines, they ate and ate. "We nearly killed ourselves eating." It took weeks of knocking about with the Federal army in Georgia before they could get transportation north. They traveled by train to Wolcott's home in Michigan where they had a "great time." Their war was over.[20]

In February 1862, Harmon Wheeler's sister Susan Austin and her husband Andrew sold the little farm that had belonged to Harmon and Harrison. The buyer was James Dingee. James was a laborer and farmer who came from Bucks County, Pennsylvania. James Dingee married his wife Susan in Westchester County in 1835 when she was fifteen. By 1862, they still had four young children at home, William, Theodore, Alfred and Sarah. There were other, older children as well. The 1850 census reported they had eleven children.

James Dingee's age was something of a mystery. The 1850 census reported that he was then forty-nine, meaning that he was born in 1801. The New York State census of 1865 claimed he had been fifty-five in 1864, which would have made his birth year 1809. When he enlisted on January 21, 1864, the army reported his age as forty-five, the maximum age for soldiers to join up. James signed on with the 16th Regiment of New York Artillery. He was at least fifty years old. The muster roll described him as five feet, five inches tall, with blue eyes, light hair and a light complexion.[21]

What would cause a man his age to leave a large family and a new farm to join the army? By 1863 and 1864, the Union army's manpower situation had worsened dramatically. Deaths, wounds, illnesses, and the harsh realities of war came home to the North. The flow of patriotic young men into the service ebbed. The government instituted an unpopular draft law. Local governments tried to meet their draft quotas by paying bounties for enlistments. A wealthy man who did not want to serve could avoid the army altogether by paying a substitute to fight in his place. It was a system that insured that the poor fought and the rich stayed home.

James Dingee may have enlisted from purely patriotic motives. But, he was not a wealthy man. He supported his family by labor and by farming a small Mountain homestead. The year 1864 was a drought year. No farmer in Dover raised spring wheat that year because of the dryness. It may be that poverty caused Dingee to become a soldier. He did receive sixty dollars "advanced bounty," and his wife applied for the balance after his death. If he was paid as a substitute, no record of it remains.[22]

Whatever caused James to leave farm and family to go to war, it was a tragic decision. He was shot through the head and killed outside Richmond, Virginia, on October 7, 1864. His unit defended an attack by Lee's forces on the Union right flank. The army reported that he was "killed at the Chapin farm...near the junction of the New Market and Darbytown roads." At the time, he was a private in a unit of "unassigned recruits." His commanding officer wrote that he had "no effects" except $5.45 worth of uniforms.[23]

Preston Mountain Blacks in the War and "Hellmira"

BY 1863, LINCOLN PONDERED OTHER MEASURES to put soldiers in the field. There were thousands of African Americans living in the north and south who might be motivated to fight the Confederacy.

> It occurred to various people in the North, starting with the President and Secretary of War, that if these black people were free and if the army was going south in order to free them, then possibly some of them could join the army themselves and do some fighting for their freedom.[24]

It was an unpopular idea at first. The soldiers of the North were no strangers to racism. But, Bruce Catton wrote, they had a saying: "A black man can stop a bullet as well as a white man." Soon, African American soldiers proved to be very good soldiers indeed. At the battles of Charleston, South Carolina, and at Petersburg and the Crater outside Richmond, colored troops fought hard and suffered high casualties. Perhaps they viewed the chance to fight in their own cause as an opportunity and an honor.[20]

Some of the descendants of the African American families of Preston Mountain (and one man who married a descendant) took advantage of this opportunity. Aaron Chapel's granddaughter

Lucy married Daniel Holdridge in 1849 in Chenango County, New York. Her father, Aaron Chapel Jr., lived with them according to the 1850 census. Daniel Holdridge served with the Union army.

Though the evidence is inconclusive, it appears that two of Prince Dunbar's great-grandsons and one husband of a great-granddaughter fought for the North. There is no doubt that George Dunbar, Milton Dunbar, and George Hector (Maria Dunbar's husband) all enlisted in the army and served. The question is whether their ancestor was Prince Dunbar.

Prince Dunbar and Ruth Dunbar, and two sons Robert and Caleb, lived on Preston Mountain prior to the federal census of 1820. That census named Ruth as the head of the family, the only Dunbar family in Dover. Robert Dunbar lost the family farm at Sheriff's Sale in 1827 (as was previously recounted). No Dunbar household appeared in Dover in the 1830 census. But, in 1840, Morris Dunbar appeared as the head of a family. Morris may have been a son of either Robert or Caleb, but there is no record confirming that. He had several children, including George, Milton, and Maria. It may be that the families of Prince and Morris Dunbar were unrelated. It seems likely, however, that they were kin. Each census from 1820 to 1860 (except 1830) included an African American family named Dunbar in the town of Dover.

At any rate, both George and Milton Dunbar enlisted in Company C of the 26th Regiment, United States Colored Infantry. They fought in South Carolina, where African American troops fought several battles. Both men survived the war. Milton died in 1907, apparently without children. He was buried in the Grand Army of the Republic Cemetery in Danbury, Connecticut.

George Dunbar lived in New Milford, Connecticut, until his death in 1919. He had several children, including a son named Martin who continued the Dunbar military tradition. France awarded Martin the Croix de Guerre for his service in World War I.[26]

Maria Dunbar's young husband, George Hector, served with

Company H of the 28th Regiment of Colored Connecticut Volunteers. The regiment fought in the area of Petersburg, Virginia, for ten months in 1864 and 1865. Hector died of typhoid at Fort Monroe, Virginia, in November 1864. His nineteen-year-old widow applied for his pension.

DISEASE WAS THE SOLDIERS' MOST DANGEROUS ENEMY, on either side, during the Civil War. "Indeed, twice as many Civil War soldiers died of disease as were killed and mortally wounded in combat." The three worst killers were dysentery, typhoid, and pneumonia. Malaria and smallpox also struck both armies.[27]

What John Wolcott learned of disease and misery in a Southern prison, his fellow mountaineer Harmon Wheeler discovered in a Northern prison—Elmira. Harmon had survived almost four full years with the New York Cavalry (he reenlisted at Culpepper, Virginia, in 1863). When his unit was mustered out in August 1865, Harmon was at Elmira, New York.

The 6th Regiment New York Cavalry fought most of their battles in Virginia, at Seven Pines and Malvern Hill. In 1862, the 6th saw action at South Mountain and Antietam, and later at Fredericksburg. In 1863, they were at Gettysburg, then back to Virginia for the Battle of the Wilderness. In 1864, the unit was part of Sheridan's Shenandoah Valley campaign. The unit's war ended at Appomatox Courthouse on April 9, 1865, when Lee surrendered. Harmon Wheeler's pension records do not report how many of these actions he saw (nor any of the scores of other confrontations of the 6th). He survived the bullets and the shells. Then he encountered Elmira.

Elmira boasted a Federal prison for Rebel troops. How or why Harmon Wheeler came to be posted there is unknown. Perhaps he accompanied a detail of prisoners. While there was probably no good time to be at Elmira, 1865 was the worst of times. Smallpox broke out there in the spring.

Almost 25 percent of the 12,123 Confederate soldiers who entered the 40-acres prisoner of war camp at Elmira, NY, died. Their death rate was more than double the average death rate in other Northern prison camps, and only 2 percent less than the death rate at the infamous Southern prison at Andersonville, GA. The deaths at Elmira were caused by diseases brought on by terrible living conditions and starvation, conditions deliberately caused by the vindictive US commissary-general of prisoners, Col. William Hoffman.[28]

The Confederate prisoners called the place "Hellmira." When their families sent them clothing to help survive the northern winter, Hoffman ordered any article that was not gray to be burned.

The Union began paroling prisoners in June 1865, beginning with the strongest and the healthiest. The last of the prisoners, those from the hospital, left the camp in August 1865, the same month that Harmon Wheeler died at Elmira.

There is a white tombstone on the west side of Valley View Cemetery in Dover Plains. The inscription on it reads:

James Dingee – Fell at the Battle of Loral
Hill, VA   10/7/1864   ae. 53 years
Died on the Field of Battle
Tis Noble Thus to Die
God Smiles on Radiant Soldiers
Their Record is on High

Chapter Fourteen
"Blowed Out For Good"

O N JULY 28, 1866, CONGRESS PASSED AN ACT providing for pensions for the veterans of the Civil War, their widows, and their children. On August 24, 1866, Susan Dingee made her mark on an application for her husband James' benefits. Susan's Mountain neighbors, Sabrina Wheeler (mother of Harmon Wheeler of Elmira) and William Wolcott (brother of John Wolcott of Andersonville) witnessed her application.[1]

Susan could not have known in 1866 that she faced nearly forty years of trouble with the US Government pension authorities. The troubles began almost immediately when the records of one James (S.) Dingee surfaced. Dr. Edward Parker of Poughkeepsie, New York, had signed a statement dated November 16, 1864, that James S. Dingee was unfit for duty by reason of "a gunshot wound in the walls of the abdomen." The report was dated five weeks after Susan's husband James was shot through the head and killed in Virginia.[2]

The government's difficulty in identifying James persisted until at least 1890. In that year, the pension records indicated that James (E.) Dingee of Co. K, 16th N.Y. Artillery, had died of "diarrhoea" on May 16, 1865. The records also showed that James Dingee had deserted from a hospital at Fort Monroe, Virginia, on November 17, 1864. The same records noted that the "Name James Dingee has not been found on a roll of Co. K, 16th N.Y. Artillery." These problems could be solved only by Susan submitting and resubmitting paperwork. Susan Dingee, of course, lived on top of the Mountain, two or three miles from the nearest post office. She was unable to read or write and she had minor children to care for, but she persisted. She did receive a pension, beginning in the 1860s, of eight dollars per month from October 7, 1864, (the date James was killed) and two dollars per month for each of her minor children commencing July 25, 1866.

According to the records, Susan's troubles were not over, however. The pension records (which are brief notes made on a piece of brown paper) reveal that the adjutant general's office revisited the issue of James' identity several times. They asked Susan to prove that she was really married to James; she had no marriage certificate. The justice of the peace in Westchester County who had married them was dead. So Susan obtained the affidavits of Amos Fuller and Obadiah Smith saying that they had attended the wedding.

In 1882, she applied for an increase in the pension on the grounds that, because of sickness and old age, she was unable to work and the pension was her only means of support. The Mountain farm had been sold in 1876; she lived on six and a half acres she owned near Dover Plains. There is a note in the adjutant general's file that Congressman John H. Ketcham (formerly John H. Ketcham, commander of the 150th New York) intervened on her behalf. Susan received an increase to twelve dollars per month. The pension was "dropped" on September 22, 1903, because Susan had died.[3]

Susan's neighbor Sabrina Wheeler also suffered in the war's aftermath. She was in her mid-sixties. She had just lost her son and she was eking out a living on a Mountain farm. The 1867 map shows that "H. Wheeler" lived on the farm in the vale just northwest of Depression Mountain (a.k.a. the "Bald Hill"). This was the same farm that Hiram's distant relative Valentine Wheeler had willed to his son John at the end of the Revolution.

But Hiram Wheeler did not own the farm; his wife Sabrina owned it. She acquired the property from Nelson Cook in 1862, although she failed to record the deed until 1865. It was unusual at that time for a married woman to take title to land, and even more unusual to take title without her husband's name on the deed. This may indicate that Hiram Wheeler was under some kind of disability. At any rate, the mapmakers of the day believed Hiram owned the farm.[4]

Hiram Wheeler died in 1867, leaving Sabrina and their youngest daughter, Eliza, by themselves. Another daughter and her husband,

Sarah and Edgar Soule, owned a farm about half a mile south (south of Depression Pond) of Sabrina. In 1867, Sabrina sold her farm to William Wolcott, and she and Eliza probably moved to the Soule farm. They are listed as living together in the 1870 census. Eliza was twenty-four years old. The Soules sold their farm to Sabrina in 1873. Thus, in a period when very few women owned real estate, Sabrina Wheeler had owned two farms.[5]

THE STATUS OF WOMEN changed in the nineteenth century. To illustrate the novelty of Sabrina Wheeler's ownership of land, consider the language of an 1816 Connecticut lawsuit:

The husband by marriage, acquires a right to the use of the real estate of his wife, during her life; and if they have a child born alive, then if he survives, during his life, as tenant by the curtesy. He acquires an absolute right to her chattels real and may dispose of them…as to the property of the wife accruing during couverture [marriage] the same rule is applicable.[6]

Lawrence Friedman, commenting on this case in *History of American Law*, wrote: "Essentially, husband and wife were one flesh; but the man was owner of that flesh."[7]

Friedman went on:

It was not usual to give women actual control over land. . . . Rather property was settled on women; or left in trust; or given to women in the form of lesser "estates": life interests for daughters, estates during widowhood for a surviving wife.[8]

Clearly this old arrangement was less than fair to women. New York passed its first Married Women's Property Law in 1848, which improved women's rights. But, as Friedman wrote: "Passage of these laws did not signal a revolution in the status of women; rather they ratified and adjusted a silent revolution." That is, the new laws made the real estate markets work better for men, too. With women included, there were more buyers and sellers.[9]

This still left the majority of wives with dismal prospects. Their husbands owned the homesteads or farms where they lived; their only claim was their "dower" interest (a fractional interest they might realize upon the death of their husbands) and an interest that left the land in the control of their sons. A man might decide to sell the farm to another, in which case his wife or mother would have to sign the deed in order to convey her dower interest. The legislature recognized the possibilities for coercion here. Early deeds all contained language in the acknowledgment signed before an officer of the court (a notary or commissioner of deeds): "and the said [Jane Doe] being by me examined privately and apart from her husband she acknowledged that she executed this deed freely without any fear of compulsion by her said Husband."

That universal language was taken from a deed from Jacob and Mary Maxum to Samuel Benson for the old John Bolt farm (now underneath Depression Pond). The Maxums apparently kept a right to part of the premises, including a part of the residence: "Also the dwelling house in which said John Bolt died being the west half with the privilege of baking in the east part and going down cellar when necessary."[10]

By 1875, Sabrina Wheeler was the head of a household consisting of her daughter Eliza, age twenty-nine, and a farm laborer, Peter Chase of Kent, age fifty. Peter was a widower with a grown son, Peter Chase Jr. Sabrina farmed forty acres of improved land with another thirty acres of woods. In 1874, they raised two acres of Indian corn and a half-acre each of potatoes and tobacco, making a total of three acres in tillage. The three of them may have worked this land entirely by hand; they owned no oxen and no horses. It is, of course, possible that a neighbor plowed their land for them with a team of horses. Nevertheless, one man and two women hoed weeds out of three acres of row crops and then harvested the crops entirely by hand. The census records indicate that they succeeded well enough that their yields per acre equaled or exceeded that of their neighbors.

In addition, Sabrina's farmstead produced forty bushels of apples from fifty trees (which was below the yields of the neighbors). They milked four cows and butchered one hog. The census valued the farm at $1,100.00 with sales of $50.00 in 1874. The buildings were worth $250.00. In economic terms, the 1875 census marked Sabrina Wheeler's farm as one of the poorest in Dover.[11]

Eventually, Eliza Wheeler married their farmhand, Peter Chase, though he was much older. By the 1880 census, Peter was the head of household; Sabrina, now seventy-five years old, lived with them. Sabrina died of old age in 1886. Her will left everything to Eliza and to Eliza's children and nothing to her other children.[12]

Peter and Eliza Chase raised a large family; they still lived on the Mountain in 1900. After Peter's death, Eliza bought the old Thomas J. Wolcott place on the hill next to Aaron Chapel's abandoned farm. She continued the hard, independent life her mother had lived.

Farming in the eastern United States suffered during the last half of the nineteenth century, particularly the last thirty years. Many causes combined to worsen conditions for agriculture in New England and New York. Among them were the drought of 1864 and 1865, the opening of cheap western lands, railroad transportation of goods to market, a series of recessions or depressions, exhausted soil, and failure of farmers to adapt to changing conditions. Howard S. Russell's history, *A Long, Deep Furrow: Three Centuries of Farming in New England*, summarized the situation in Chapter 31, entitled "Discouragement:"

> The thirty years that followed 1870, including as they did the panic of 1873, seem to have been the most difficult that New England farmers had faced since Shay's Rebellion. "Decades of almost unrelieved gloom," a writer on Connecticut calls them. Prices of many staples, especially grains, were in almost continuous decline from peaks reached at war's end, as cheap western grain, helped by railroad rate cuts, flooded in.... By 1876 the corn harvested in a town like Rochester, New Hampshire, was only a little over half what its farmers had husked a quarter-century earlier, and small grains had all but disappeared there.
>
> New England's wool shearings decreased one sixth between 1870 and 1880. By 1900 they were only two thirds those of 1870 and never again reached a total of real importance.[13]

The number of farms overall began to decline by 1880 and the number of vacant or abandoned farms increased.

> It was the young in particular who took off. In 1871 at Northfield, Massachusetts, a group of ex-soldiers organized, sent a scout to spy

152

out land in the New West, and planned to move as a body to settle there.[14]

Russell concludes: "with sheep herding unprofitable and cattle prices low, decade by decade the poorer, stonier, frostier hill farms went relentlessly back to the woodland for which nature designed them."[15]

All these factors applied to Preston Mountain. But a unique condition existed there; a century of charcoal-making aggravated conditions on the Mountain. Because the New York State census reports of 1865 and 1875 contained voluminous agricultural statistics, it is possible to examine the nature of farming on the Mountain and compare it to farming elsewhere in Dover.

The Appendix lists seven farmers from Dover and the statistics of their agricultural means and production as shown by the 1865 and 1875 census reports. Four of these men farmed on Preston Mountain: Henry J. Hufcut, Allen P. Kennedy, Clark Preston (and later, his grandson Preston Hufcut), and William Woolcott (Wolcott). The three remaining farmers, Jacob V. Dutcher, Sherman S. Tabor, and Jacob Senk, farmed off the Mountain. They were chosen because it was possible to identify the locations of their farms, and because they exemplified the diversity of farms in the town.

Henry J. Hufcut inherited his 320-acre place high on the Mountain near the Connecticut line. His grandfather George Hufcut, the lawyer, acquired the property in increments beginning in the 1820s. The place consisted mostly of the earlier, smaller farms of the Hill, Dunbar, and Jackson families who had first homesteaded it. Henry was twenty-one in 1865.

Allen P. Kennedy inherited his farm of 150 acres from his great-uncle David Preston, Martin's son, who had farmed it since before the Revolution. Allen Kennedy was forty-seven in 1865.

Clark Preston acquired his 170 acres from his mother Annis, after his father Philip died young. Clark began farming at a young age—he recorded his earmark when he was twelve years old. His farm was next door to Allen Kennedy's. Clark and Allen were second cousins. Their two houses are the only dwellings of the Preston Mountain com-

The Clark Preston house.

munity that remain today. Clark was sixty-seven years old in 1865. He died before 1875, and his grandson Preston Hufcut ran the farm, though Luna Preston, Clark's widow owned it. The farm included the old homestead of Enoch Philleo.

William Wolcott owned 260 acres in 1865, but he doubled his acreage over the next ten years. By 1875, he farmed 500 acres after a fashion. He was thirty-three years old in 1865, and he and his wife Mary were raising a large family. Like Hufcut, Kennedy, and Preston, Wolcott farmed a place that had been farmed for a century or more. Significantly (and alone among the four named farmers) Wolcott listed his occupation as "farmer and collier." The other men called themselves simply, "farmers."[16]

Jacob V. Dutcher's farm in the valley was nearest to the Mountain. It lay at the base of Preston Mountain on the east side of the TenMile River just south of the junction of Sand Hill Road and Berkshire Road. Jacob owned 153 acres in 1865 and 125 acres in 1875. The land was about equally divided between hilly pasture/meadow and river bottom or river terrace.[17]

Sherman S. Tabor's 116 acres most nearly resembled the land on the Mountain, occupying the northeast flank of West Mountain west of the Stone Church Brook. Though much of the land was steep and stony, Tabor's predecessors cleared two large tracts at the very crest of the ridge. Like most of the Chestnut Ridge neighborhood, which it bordered, this high land boasted deep and productive soil. Most of Tabor's farm has grown back to brush and forest. The outbuildings are gone, but the old farmhouse is still lived in.

Jacob Senk's name does not appear in the 1865 census. He emigrated from Germany before 1875. His farm, as describe in the 1875 census, was one of the largest (330 acres) and most successful in Dover. High on Chestnut Ridge, it is still farmed today by Albert Soukup Jr.

The farmers themselves provided the information for each census. There is enough uniformity, in terms of yields, values, and acreage, to suggest that the information was generally accurate. However, there were some entries that seemed excessive.

The most striking factor in the census records was the ratio of improved land to woodland on the various farms. On Preston Mountain, the woodlots were much larger than the pasture and plow land (except for Kennedy, whose ratio was even). The other farmers all maintained significantly more improved land than forest. In 1875, William Wolcott owned 400 acres of woods and 100 acres of improved land, of which he plowed only 10 acres. Jacob Senk, on the other hand, kept only 75 acres of woodland; the balance of his farm was 305 acres of meadow, pasture, and tillage. He plowed 38 acres. Obviously, Wolcott and Senk ran totally different ventures.

In the nineteenth century, "power" meant human or animal muscle. In 1865, three of the four Preston Mountain farms worked a yoke of oxen each. The other farms used horses. By 1875, none of the farms kept oxen. That year, Preston Hufcut apparently worked his farm with neither horses nor oxen. He reported that he'd plowed twelve acres. His neighbor, Allen Kennedy, must have done it for him.

Sheep began to play a larger role on the Mountain farms by 1875. Wolcott owned forty-two head and Hufcut kept thirty. They both sheared their animals for wool. Sheep were notorious for the damage their grazing caused; they nibbled the grass down to the roots. On the eroded Mountain soil, the sheep may have hastened the ultimate end of the farms. By contrast, neither Dutcher, Tabor, nor Senk owned a single sheep.

The dairy business clearly increased the cash income of those who tried it. Dutcher, for example, increased his herd from eight cows in 1865 to thirty-seven in 1875. His income doubled. Jacob Senk ran a herd of sixty-three cows in 1875, and his $3,600.00 of income was among the highest in Dover. Sherman Tabor had no milk cows.

The men on Preston Mountain owned a handful of cows, probably enough for their own milk, butter, and cheese. They lived hours away from the new railroad that stretched up through the valley in 1850. Farmers with access to the railhead had an advantage. They could ship their products to New York City markets.

A comparison of yields leads to the conclusion that Mountain land was less fertile than elsewhere in the town. Hay production in 1865 was poor everywhere because of the drought. Small grains would not grow that year. In 1875, none of the Mountain farms produced hay crops in excess of one and a half tons per acre. Tabor and Dutcher put up more than 2 tons per acre that year. Senk maintained more than 180 acres of meadow, a massive amount for those times. He put 200 tons in his mow, only 1.1 tons per acre. It may be, given the vast acreage he worked, that Senk had time for only one cutting that year.

Someone, either the farmers or the census takers, placed an overall value on each farm, as well as a value for the buildings and the stock. By deducting the latter two figures from the overall value, it is possible to calculate an estimate of the worth of the land alone for each farm in 1875. The results are startling. Wolcott's farm was worth $7.00 an acre; Hufcut's $3.00; Kennedy's $15.00; Preston Hufcut's $15.00; Tabor's $38.00; Dutcher's $32.00; and Senk's $80.00 per acre. The Mountain land was worth only a fraction of the land off the Mountain.

The values for Preston Mountain land revealed by the census are borne out by actual purchase prices from the same period. In the decade between 1865 and 1875, William Wolcott made several purchases of land near his farm amounting to 240 acres, all woodland. In 1867, he bought 129 acres from James Ketcham for $1,300.00—$10.00 per acre. In 1869, he purchased three lots totaling 91 acres from the Edmonds family for $1,000.00—$6.00 per acre. Wolcott continued these purchases after 1875, adding 38 acres from Ebenezer Preston (Martin's grandson). All these parcels were on Preston Mountain.[19]

Wolcott's acquisitions raise questions. Where did he get the money? In 1875, he reported farm income of fifty dollars. He must have had another source of income. The second question is why did he accumulate all that cheap land? The answer to both questions is suggested by Wolcott's occupation as reported in the census; William Wolcott was a collier, first and foremost. He bought used-up farms for fuel wood for his charcoal business. Farming was a sideline for him.

The other Preston Mountain farmers were colliers as well, though perhaps not in Wolcott's class. Henry J. Hufcut sold charcoal in Kent. His son (also named Henry) recalled riding to the Kent iron furnace when he was a child. Allen P. Kennedy was noted as a careful workman who never let his charcoal wagons break down. In the late nineteenth century, charcoal was probably the principle crop of the Mountain farms. But there was no entry for "charcoal" in the census reports.[20]

The demand for charcoal disappeared at about this time. Both the furnaces at Macedonia and Bull's Bridge had shut down by 1879. The furnace at Kent closed in 1892. William Trapp Hopson described the demise of the iron industry around the Mountain.[21]

> Volume of Pennsylvania and southern irons had grown enormously, dwarfing the output of charcoal iron furnaces into a fraction of the total iron output of the country. . . . In manpower coke costs less than charcoal, takes up less room and will melt faster, without adding much if any carbon to the iron. Charcoal iron was probably selling at that time at about $40.00 per ton, while southern iron could be bought for $20.00. . . .
>
> In consequence, one after another Housatonic Valley Furnace "blowed out for good."[21]

When the furnaces died, the little community on Preston Mountain was destined to follow.

Chapter Fifteen
"The End of an Era"

THE LONG, SLOW POPULATION DECLINE on Preston Mountain became precipitous after the Civil War. From a peak of thirty families living there from 1800 to 1830, the number of households declined to twenty in 1860, fifteen in 1880, and ten by 1900. Though the median age of the population remained low because of the large size of the families, the heads of family gentrified. In 1880, they included Abijah Patchin's widow, Rebecca, age eighty-five; Edwin Patchin age sixty-one; Allen Kennedy age sixty-two; Luna Preston (Clark's widow) age seventy-five.

Bradford and Frances Thorpe headed one of the largest families reported in the 1875 federal census. Bradford, age forty-two, was listed as a collier, as was his eldest son, Edward, age nineteen. Twelve of the Thorpe's nineteen children still lived with them. Some of their babies had died young. A century later, Erroll Hufcut, grandson of Henry J. Hufcut, related a story about a woman, presumably Frances Thorpe:[1]

> Religious or not, the mountain people were hardy folk. There was a woman named Thorpe who lived on the mountain, Hufcut said. She had 18 children. . . . She had been down in the valley one day before her last child was born. Returning up the mountain side on foot, labor overtook her. She stopped and gave birth to the child, placing it in her apron. Then she continued her climb.[2]

According to one old map, the Thorpes lived on the farm once owned by Harmon and Harrison Wheeler, and later by James Dingee—another large family on the small place. At some point, the

Thorpes moved to a two hundred acre farm south of present Depression Pond, which the Soule family owned. In 1899, Millard and Cora Soule of Kent sold the "farm where Bradford Thorpe now lives" to Bradford's wife, Frances. This was the second time in the Mountain's history that a woman acquired a farm in her own name while her husband was living with her.[3]

In 1904, Frances deeded the farm to her children Edward and Julia, who immediately leased it back to both parents for life. This unusual transaction seems to have been aimed at avoiding having Bradford's name on the deed, even though the deed and lease both referred to the premises as "the place where Bradford Thorpe now lives." Bradford may have had some disability, or his creditors may have been hounding him. Whatever the reason, he never owned his home.[4]

Julia Thorpe moved off the Mountain to earn a living. In 1880, when she was twenty years old, she worked as a servant in a hotel in Poughkeepsie. Milton and Horatio Bain owned the hotel. Horatio owned a farm near Dover. Julia made an impression on the authors' mother, who remembered Julia living next door to her grandparents. "Jule" Thorpe was a tiny lady who sat on her front porch rocking and smoking a pipe. Her feet only touched the floor on the forward rocks.[5]

Peter and Eliza Chase still farmed on the Mountain in 1900. Peter was eighty years old and Eliza was sixty-two. Three children still lived with them, including their fifteen-year-old son Charles. Peter's eighty-two-year old brother, Wheaton Dutcher Chase, had also moved in with them.

Peter and Wheaton Chase's mother was Sylvia Dutcher, whose father, Cornelius Dutcher, owned a farm near the Mountain in Dover. Wheaton's son, Ransom Chase, married Sabrina Wheeler's granddaughter, Abigail Soule. Two of Wheaton Dutcher Chase's grandsons, Sherman Chase and Edwin Chase, would play important roles in the closing years of the Preston Mountain story, though neither of them ever lived on the Mountain.[6]

After Peter died, Eliza continued to farm on the Mountain. In 1919, she bought a fifty-three-acre farm that had once belonged to Thomas J. Wolcott. It was high on the hill just east of the abandoned homestead of Aaron Chapel. Eliza was almost eighty. Foster Richards of South

Kent remembered encountering Eliza when he was a boy (around 1913).

> Sixty years ago, when I was 16. [written in 1973] I walked across the mountain from Dover home to Kent. On the way over I came on Aunt Liza Chase out haying. She lived next door to where my mother was born. [Richard's mother was Louise Soule] I stopped and gave her a hand with the haying. . . ?[7]

Aunt Liza Chase would have been about seventy-five years old that day when she was out haying—Sabrina's rugged daughter to the end.

Allen P. Kennedy died in 1889 at age seventy-two. He had farmed and made charcoal on the Mountain all his life. He and his wife, Frances Ann, raised four daughters and three sons. They named one boy "Martin." All of the children lived at home according to the 1870 census. Four of them listed their occupations as "schoolteacher."

The Preston Mountain school, established in 1820, was reputed to be the first public school in Dover. It brought change to the Mountain people. Where the parents could not read or sign their names, the children became educated people. The families welcomed the school and its teachers. Arthur T. Benson, a Dover man, recalled his days as a teacher there:

> In the winter of 1880 the writer taught there. Sixteen pupils were registered. Among others who had their first experience of teaching school in that little weather- beaten school house nestling in a shelter of the woods near the highway, were John A. Bangs, of the New York Custom House, and Frank Connell, but recently retired after many years of services at the 34th Street branch of the New York post office. The salary was two dollars a week and board. We "boarded around" two weeks at a place in succession. The hospitality was unexcelled, the cuisine above criticism and the big feather beds an invitation to calm repose, undisturbed by the Wintry blasts that swept over the mountain.[8]

No school records remain—no record of when it stopped educating pupils. By 1900, there were only a handful of children living on the Mountain. When the students stopped coming, the building began to deteriorate. Sherman Chase of Kent revisited the site, probably in the 1940s.

> Fifty years later I went by that schoolhouse on Preston Mountain. The roof had fallen in but the sides were still standing. The site had shown the wear and tear of time but the stone steps that went up to the entrance door were just the same as ever.[9]

The school lot.

In 1973, Alison Birch saw the same scene. "The supporting beams lie criss-crossed on the ground, and the cellar hole is filled with the leaves and branch bits dropped here by the winds that have traveled the mountain ridge throughout the century since children gathered for their classes." By 2004, nothing remained of the school.[10] The buildings were disappearing. By the 1920s, most of the mountain residents were gone too. Only Erben Kennedy remained.

In *The History of Dover Township*, there is a photograph, probably taken in the early 1920s, of six men and a dog. Five of the men were respected citizens down in Dover Plains: H. S. Benson, the school principal; Joe Humeston, the constable; Ed Haggerty, a real estate broker; Tom Boyce, a war veteran and future bank president; and "Goldie"

Bangs, a war veteran and friend to all. Sitting erect on a log in their midst was a lean old man, Erben Kennedy. He was then about seventy-five years old. There is a stone wall in the background—a wall on Erben's farm. All of the men in the photo hold axes; they were there to help the old man cut his winter wood supply.[11]

Erben Kennedy was the last descendant of Martin and Rebecca Preston to live on the Mountain. His brothers and sisters moved off to become teachers and to start new lives. Erben never married. One suspects that he had a speech impediment, since his given name, according to the 1870 federal census, was "Irving." "Erben" may have been his way of saying "Irving." In any event, though he was something of a hermit, Erben was a popular man. As told in the Preface, all who visited the Mountain in the twentieth century sought him out, and all were welcomed.

Erben's mother was born Frances Ann Patchin, daughter of Eli Patchin. *The History and Genealogy of the Patchin/Patchen Family* contains a description of Erben and his life on the Mountain, written by Annie L. Waldron:

> Erben Kennedy, a bachelor, was willed the farm on the mountain which he loved, when the family moved into Connecticut, together with the horses, cows, chickens and young stock. A tidy housekeeper, he was a very good cook, and he had many visitors from Dover who went hunting, especially over the weekends, bringing their own provisions. Well educated and a good entertainer, Erben was a splendid host, and they had glorious times.
>
> Cherries, peaches and huckleberries grew in abundance on his farm, which his sisters and niece would preserve for him; they visited him twice a month, with the makings of a Sunday dinner and enough food to last a few days.
>
> Twice a year they would clean house, which gesture he did not seem to appreciate, saying he "wished the women folks would let his things alone, never could find anything when they were through." Nevertheless, it was a devoted family, and later in life he used to come down from the mountain with his faithful horse, Daisy, to spend the winters with his sisters and brother.[12]

Sherman Chase also stopped in to visit Erben.

One day I went over to Mr. Kennedy's to get some water. This was in the summertime and of course we were helping at the mill. [The Chase family cut and milled railroad ties on the Mountain]. In front of the door was a big flat stone. I walked up pretty close and I saw this big [rattle]snake lying right across the stone. I jumped back and it didn't stir or anything.

About then Mr. Kennedy came around the corner. He said, "M'boy, did you want something?"

"Yes, I came over to get some water to drink. The brook down there has gone dry." And I says," There's an awful big snake on your stone step."

"Oh," he says," don't let that bother you. As long as you don't bother him he won't bother you. . . . I'll get your water. . . ."

When he went in the snake didn't seem to bother him. He just simply stepped around the snake a little and handed me the jug.[13]

Alone on the Mountain in 1922, Erben Kennedy mowed weeds from the cemetery, entertained guests, and rusticated. Arthur T. Benson wrote, "Mr. Kennedy seems saddened by the great change on the mountain in recent years. The neighbors and companions of his youth and middle life are all gone. The land has passed into non-resident ownership."[14]

Erben sold his father's farm to Claire Hilton of Brooklyn, New York, in 1914. Hilton also bought the farms that had belonged to Clark Preston and Bradford Thorpe. Erben Kennedy remained on the Mountain in a house south of his parents' place.[15]

By the 1920s, others were buying up Mountain land. Sherman Chase's brother Edwin began acquiring land as trustee for the Preston Mountain Club of New Haven, Connecticut. He purchased the Wolcott farm in 1909. In 1924, Chase bought the 315-acre Hufcut farm from the heirs of Edwin Vincent of Dover, who had foreclosed on it. Raymond Gerard also bought land for the club. In 1925, the club leased hunting rights on the old Abel Rust farm from James Bates. It also acquired the six hundred acres of the original Schaghticoke reservation that Ebenezer Preston Jr. had bought in 1801.[16]

Eliza Chase died in 1925. Her heirs found it impossible to agree on the distribution of the fifty-three acre farm she had owned. They filed a partition action in the Dutchess County Supreme Court seeking help in dividing the property. In 1926, the referee in the action sold the farm to the Preston Mountain Club. By the time the Great Depression struck, the club was the largest landowner on the Mountain.[17]

The Crane family of Dover and New Haven, Connecticut, also acquired large pieces of the mountain, mostly on either side of Kennedy Bridge Brook. The family built a high stone dam on the brook. They backed it up in its narrow valley for more than a mile, forming Crane Pond.[18]

During the Great Depression, the Cranes and the Preston Mountain Club hired Sherman Chase to build log cabins for them. Later in life, he guessed that he had built at least twenty-six cabins (not all on the Mountain). The first cabins were for Fred Williams and A.C. Gilbert, the founders of the club. Then he built a cabin for Theodore and Donald Crane on the rocky edge of Crane Pond. Chase also built camps for the club on the hill south of Duck Pond and north of Depression Pond. Chase used straight hemlock logs. One cabin boasted chestnut paneling cut from first growth trees logged on the Schaghticokes' land.[19]

Other people built more primitive camps on some of the abandoned farms. From the 1930s to the present, hunting has been the principle occupation. Except for a handful of homes on South East Mountain Road, there were no longer any permanent residents. The farms grew back to forest and the buildings collapsed or burned. Only two homes from the old community remain, those of Clark Preston and Allen P. Kennedy.

With the deaths of Erben Kennedy and Eliza Chase in 1924 and 1925, the last of the old Preston Mountain families disappeared from the Mountain. Annie K. Waldron wrote their epitaph:

> Erben Kennedy's passing closed the last link in the chain of old families who once formed an industrious, frugal and populous community, who spun and wove their cloth, both woolen and linen, made their dyes, dipped candles, wove rag carpets, held apple peeling bees and quilting bees. Flour, sugar and fish were brought in by the barrel, and a cheese room lined with shelves was filled with various sizes and shapes of cheeses and great churns for making butter.

Geese were raised for pillows and featherbeds, and sheep for wool. The charcoal pits kept the men busy day and night, used for the pig iron furnaces, a hard endless toil which they loved and enjoyed. The end of an era.[20]

Legacy

PRESTON MOUNTAIN evolved from wilderness back to wilderness in less than two centuries. To call what remains of the community a "ghost town"—stone walls, cellar holes, and a cemetery—is to acknowledge the missing humanity there. Generations lived and died on the Mountain, hundreds of people—none remain.

The transformation from first-growth chestnut and oak forest, through complete deforestation in the nineteenth century, to oak forest today, has been nearly complete. Stately trees still grow there. In the summer, when foliage is thick, remnants of human habitation can be hard to find. The people left little of themselves.

Even in the cemetery the barriers of time fall between our generation and theirs. Dozens of unmarked stones protrude from the ground. Some have been rudely carved with tombstone "shoulders," but the names and vital dates of the dead are no longer legible, if, indeed, they were ever carved there in the first place.

There were more than thirty households during the early nineteenth century. Today, one can find physical evidence of no more than fifteen homes. This testifies to the poverty of the pioneers; some of them built rude huts without stone improvements. If they fenced their livestock, they used wood rails or brush. Decay and fallen leaves have erased all evidence of these folks.

It is tempting to think of Preston Mountain as a refuge—a place where people retreated as a last resort. The Schaghticokes retreated to their hillside enclave from New Milford and Pish-goch-ti-goch and elsewhere, driven there by white encroachment. The African Americans probably had nowhere else to go. If their farms were remote, they were at least farms that others had not previously claimed (except, perhaps, Captain Abraham Fuller). The Yankees were "poor and dispossessed" squatters on the last available frontier in the mid-eighteenth century. Colonial America offered little opportunity for most people. The Mountain pioneers recognized their chance to grab land in the title vacuum caused by the division of the Oblong. They moved in, cleared the forest, planted crops, and built homes. When powerful New Yorkers evicted the first wave of settlers, others followed.

They had grit. Despite the competing claims of William Smith, Esq., and the Church of England, and despite the ruthless quelling of the Anti-Rent Rebellion, Martin Preston and his fellow settlers stuck. Their petitions to the colony defied the claims of Smith, while pretending to recognize them. Many settlers enlisted in the rebel cause in the Revolution and risked everything. Their boldness paid off; the Revolution removed their competition and effectively settled the land claims. Several generations clung to the land, some remaining in the smoke of their chimneys beyond the patience of their children. Those who stayed labored hard on the stony farmsteads.

Mountain people cherished their standing as citizens in the new country. From the first Dover town meeting in 1807, men from Preston Mountain attended, voted, and were elected to office, regardless of their color. They enlisted to fight in the wars. Most of them suffered, and some died, from soldiering. Without exception, military service left the veterans poor.

They were tolerant of newcomers. Abijah Patchin and Ezekiel Thayer kept going with the help of loans from Martin Preston. All the evidence indicates that the African American families fit into their community around them. Tolerance extended even to former enemies. Though William Bradshaw fought for the British, he returned to the Mountain, married a minuteman's sister, and socialized with his former enemy.

The iron industry overwhelmed the Mountain. Subsistence farmers turned to harvesting and burning the forest for their livelihoods, thereby losing control of their fates. A small number of capitalists controlled the iron companies. The industry was totally dependent on wood. When iron makers in Pennsylvania and elsewhere switched to coal, iron masters in Connecticut and New York could not compete. The woodcutters, colliers, and teamsters were out of work.

From 1766 to 1924, the people of Preston Mountain were people of the past. Their lives were not like our lives. They farmed by hand or with beasts. Gasoline engines and electricity never reached them. They cooked and heated with wood fires. They piped water from a spring or dipped it from a well. They relieved themselves in outhouses. Most had large families and lived with three generations to a house. They delivered their own babies, nursed their own suffering, and buried their own dead. Despite all their hardships, many lived to a great old age. Only train whistles from the valley and smoke from iron furnaces intruded on a world that was not far different from life in the middle ages.

In the twentieth century, people in Kent and Dover demonstrated growing interest in the Mountain and its people. Genealogies and newspaper articles praised the attractions of the simple life there, and people made pilgrimages to experience it. Their stories reflect the gentleness and hospitality of the Mountain folk, and, paradoxically, their rugged independence. Erben Kennedy attracted bright and vigorous people to his home. Perhaps they sensed in this man a disappearing world—a world where an honest, self-sufficient man could be at home with the land, with all living creatures, and with himself.

APPENDIX

	Henry Hufcut	A.P. Kennedy	Clark Preston	Wm. Wolcott
1865 improved land (acres)	100	70	100	100
1875 improved land (acres)	100	75	60	100
1865 timber (acres)	200	80	70	160
1875 timber (acres)	330	75	100	400
1865 farm value	$2,000	$2,000	$1,700	$3,000
1875 farm value	$2,000	$3,000	$3,000	$5,000
1875 hay (tons)	35	42	20	20
1875 corn (bushels)	50	150	100	75
1875 apples (bushels)	200	75	300	150
1875 potatoes (bushels)	60	100	50	40
1875 cows	5	4	-	6
1875 horses	1	5	-	2
1865 oxen	3	2	-	2
1875 oxen	-	-	-	-
1865 sheep	11	11	10	-
1875 sheep	18	-	-	24
1875 farm sales	$2,500	$235	$100	$50

	J. V. Dutcher	S.S. Tabor	Jacob Senk
1865 improved land (acres)	80	80	-
1875 improved land (acres)	80	80	305
1865 timber (acres)	75	36	-
1875 timber (acres)	45	36	75
1865 farm value	$5,000	$5,225	-
1875 farm value	$6,000	$5,500	$35,000
1875 hay (tons)	50	60	200
1875 corn (bushels)	200	400	180
1875 apples (bushels)	100	50	300
1875 potatoes (bushels)	100	125	200

1875 cows	37	-	63
1875 horses	2	2	4
1865 oxen	-	-	-
1875 oxen	-	-	-
1865 sheep	-	-	-
1875 sheep	-	-	-
1875 farm sales	$1,400	$500	$3,600

Endnotes

PREFACE

1. *Poughkeepsie Sunday Courier*, November 12, 1922, p. 1.
2. Turner, Frederick Jackson, *Frontier & Section: Selected Essays*, Englewood Cliffs, NJ, Prentice-Hall, Inc., 1961, p. 14.

CHAPTER ONE: PRESTON MOUNTAIN TODAY

1. Wolf Swamp, Office of the Dutchess County Clerk, Deed Liber 27, p. 194.
2. Deeds mentioning chestnuts, Office of the Dutchess County Clerk; Deed Liber 50, p. 10; Deed Liber 25, p. 226; Deed Liber 66, p. 11.
3. Leggett, *Patchin Family*, p. 619.

CHAPTER TWO: A MIGHTY HUNTER

1. Marriages, Kent Vital Statistics, Office of the Kent Town Clerk.
2. Home location and type. Drawing on survey map of Lands of Martin Preston in author's possession.
3. "Chestnuts," Wright, Karen, *Discover Magazine*, vol. 25, no. 5, May 2004, p. 59.
4. Preston, *Descendants of Roger Preston*, p. 93.
5. Ibid., p. 94–95.
6. Public Records of Connecticut, p. 108.
7. Parkman, *Montcalm & Wolfe*, p. 240.
8. Sedgwick, *History of Sharon*, p. 40.
9. Ibid., p. 40.
10. Parkman, *Montcalm & Wolfe*, p. 154.
11. Doherty, *Settlers*, vol. I, p. 410, 475.
12. Doherty, *Settlers*, vol. IV, p. 19.
13. Preston, *Descendants of Roger Preston*, p. 5.
14. Ibid., p. 12.
15. "Salem Witch Trials Documentary Archive and Transcription Project of the University of Virginia website at http://etext.virginia.edu/salem/witchcraft/archives/essex/.
16. Ibid.
17. Roach, *The Salem Witch Trials*, p. 106.

CHAPTER THREE: THE OBLONG AND THE HOVEOUT LANDS

1. Survey map of lands of Martin Preston in author's possession.
2. Deed, Nathan Soule to Prince Dunbar, Office of the Dutchess County Clerk, Deed Liber 18, p. 380.
3. Deed, Nathan Hoyt to Martin Preston, Office of the Kent Town Clerk, Deed Liber 7, p. 365.
4. Polhemus, *History of Dover*, p. 8–9.
5. Kim, *Landlord and Tenant*, p. 368.
6. Mark, *Agrarian Conflicts*, p. 19.
7. Ibid., p. 19.
8. Ibid., p. 31.
9. Kammen, *Colonial New York*, p. 71.
10. Mark, *Agrarian Conflicts*, p. 43.
11. MacCracken, *Old Dutchess Forever*, 140 et seq.
12. Regents, eds., *Boundaries*, p. 364.
13. MacCracken, *Old Dutchess Forever*, p. 142.
14. Ibid., p. 147.
15. Colden, Cadwallader, Map of the Oblong, New York, Original at New-York Historical Society.
16. Tancret & Rogers deed, Land papers of the State of New York, New York State Archives.
17. Antoine Tancret information from Meredith Gibson of Toncray Family Genealogy Forum.
18. Reed, *History of Amenia*, p. 92.
19. MacCracken, *Old Dutchess Forever*, p. 147.
20. Kempe Letter to Mr. Farquaharson, New-York Historical Society, William Kempe Papers, Box 6.
21. New York Indorsed Land Papers, vol. XIV, p. 262.
22. Public Records of Connecticut, May 1752, p. 108.
23. Colden, Cadwallader, Map of the Oblong, New York, New-York Historical Society.
24. Kammen, *Colonial New York*, p. 293.
25. New-York Historical Society, "The Colden Papers," p. 132.
26. Shecter, *Battle for New York*, p. 13.
27. New York Indorsed Land Papers, vol. XLII, p. 728.
28. Ibid., p. 728.
29. Deed, Ambrose Benson to Daniel Lake, Office of the Dutchess County Clerk, Deed Liber 9, p. 461.

CHAPTER FOUR: NEIGHBORS AND TENANTS REVOLT

1. Polhemus, *History of Dover*, p. 8.
2. Ibid., p. 8.
3. Ibid., p. 8.
4. Doherty, *Settlers*, vol. I, p. 704.
5. Polhemus, *History of Dover*, p. 12.
6. Doherty, *Settlers*, vol. I, p. 98.
7. Deed, Winegar to Rust, Office of the Kent Town Clerk, Deed Liber 6, p. 258; Atwater, *History of Kent*, p. 114.
8. Hopson, ed., *Iron Fever*, p. 1, 13, 25.
9. Atwater, *History of Kent*, p. 49.
10. Ibid., p. 68.
11. Ibid., p. 51.
12. Wojciechowski, *Ethnohistory*, p. 90.
13. "Trading," Store Ledgers at Kent Historical Society.
14. Orcutt, *Indians*, p. 197.
15. Ibid., p. 197.
16. Wojciechowski, *Ethnohistory*, p. 92.
17. Ibid., p. 92.
18. Ibid., Appendix D, p. 258.
19. Wilson, *Quaker Hill*, p. 35.
20. Daniel Merritt Store Ledgers, Quaker Hill Historical Society Collection.
21. Doherty, *Settlers*, vol. I, p. 383.
22. Moulton, *John Woolman*, p. 116; Wilson, *Quaker Hill*, p. 25.
23. Atwater, *History of Kent*, p. 60.
24. Lynd, *Anti-Federalism*, p. 47.
25. Ibid., p. 49.
26. Mark, *Agrarian Conflicts*, p. 94.
27. Lynd, *Anti-Federalism,* p. 50.
28. Ibid., p. 50.
29. Mark, *Agrarian Conflicts*, p. 144.
30. Ibid., p. 147.
31. Ibid., p. 147.
32. Ibid., p. 149.
33. Doherty, *Settlers*, vol. I, p. 329.

CHAPTER FIVE: THE POOR AND DISTRESSED

1. Calendar of New York Indorsed Land Papers, February 12, 1772, p. 554.
2. Ibid., p. 554.

3. Ibid., March 17, 1772, p. 50.
4. Rust, *Rust Family*, p. 105.
5. Rust marriage, Kent Vital Statistics; Sawmill, see Note 7, Chapter Three.
6. Preston, *Descendants of Roger Preston*, p. 94; Griffen and Alegre, *Wolcott Genealogy*, p. 359.
7. Fernow's Calendar of Wills, #2096, p. 473.
8. "Earmarks," Town of Dover Meeting Minutes, transcription in authors' possession.
9. De Crevecoeur, *Letters*, p. 312.
10. Ibid., p. 277.
11. Van Hoosear, *Fillow-Philleo*, p. 49.
12. Ibid., p. 49.
13. Office of the Dutchess County Clerk, Deed Liber 92, p. 526.
14. "Bradshaw Lands," Office of the Dutchess County Clerk, Deed Liber 55, p. 230.
15. Preston, *Descendants of Roger Preston*, p. 94.
16. De Crevecoeur, *Letters*, p. 59.
17. Preston, *Descendants of Roger Preston*, p. 95.

CHAPTER SIX: THE REVOLUTION
TO SUPPRESS THE INTERNAL FOES

1. Doherty, *Settlers*, vol. I, p. 412.
2. Ibid., p. 413.
3. Abel Rust Pension Application.
4. Martin, *Revolutionary Soldier*, p. 22.
5. Ibid., p. 42.
6. Rust, *Rust Family*, p. 169.
7. Scheer & Rankin, *Rebels and Redcoats*, p. 110.
8. Smith, *History of Dutchess County*, p. 159.
9. Doherty, *Settlers*, vol. I, p. 466.
10. Ibid., p. 472; Enoch Phileo Pension Application.
11. Enoch Phileo Pension Application.
12. Van Hoosear, *Fillow-Philleo*, 67 et seq.
13. Doherty, *Settlers*, vol. I, p. 472.
14. Ibid., p. 472.
15. Ibid., p. 469.
16. Ibid., p. 433.
17. Ibid., p. 469.
18. Martin, *Revolutionary Soldier*, p. 55.

19. Doherty, *Settlers*, vol. I, p. 284.
20. Ibid., p. 590–591.
21. Ibid., p. 590.
22. Wilson, *Quaker Hill*, p. 59.
23. Ibid., p. 58.
24. Doherty, *Settlers*, vol. I, p. 585.
25. Ibid., p. 585.
26. Fernow's Calendar of Wills, #2096, p. 473.

CHAPTER SEVEN: WORTHLESS CONTINENTAL MONEY

1. Martin, *Revolutionary Soldier*, p. 247.
2. Ibid., p. 242.
3. Van Hoosear, *Fillow-Philleo*, p. 50.
4. Martin, *Revolutionary Soldier*, p. 240.
5. Office of the Dutchess County Clerk, Deed Liber 55, p. 230.
6. Van Hoosear, *Fillow-Philleo*, p. 50.
7. Ibid., p. 50.
8. Ibid., p. 50.
9. Ibid., p. 48.
10. Kent Deed Book 6, p. 285.
11. Kent Deed Book 20, p. 658.
12. Abel Rust Pension Application.
13. Rust, *Rust Family*, p. 169.
14. Ibid., p 169.
15. New York Land Papers, vol. XLII, p. 158.
16. Ibid., p 158.
17. Doherty, *Settlers*, vol. I, p. 115.

CHAPTER EIGHT: ALL OTHER FREE PEOPLE

1. Wood, *Radicalism*, p. 186.
2. Doherty, *Settlers*, vol. I, p. 328.
3. Doherty, *Settlers*, vol. I, p. 809.
4. Ibid., vol. VI, p. 463–464.
5. Sharon Vital Statistics.
6. Feder, *Village of Outcasts*, p. 27.
7. Seymour, *Barzillai Slosson*, p. 18.
8. Doherty, *Settlers*, vol. IV, p. 512.
9. Office of the Dutchess County Clerk, Deed Liber 18, p. 380.
10. Doherty, *Settlers*, vol. I, p. 305.

11. Office of the Dutchess County Clerk, Deed Liber 18, p. 380.
12. Johnson, *Kent Families*, (No page number); Atwater, *History of Kent*, p. 77–78.
13. Atwater, *History of Kent*, Page 77–78.
14. Benson, *Jacob Benson*, p. 119.
15. "Tax List or Assessment Roll of Pawlingstown in the County of Dutchess for the year 1801."
16. Minutes of Dover Town Meetings. Transcript in author's possession, pages not numbered.
17. Ibid., pages not numbered.
18. Benson, *Jacob Benson*, p. 119.
19. Orcutt, *Indians*, p. 200.
20. Public Records of the State of Connecticut, vol. X, p. 249.

CHAPTER NINE: THE SCATACOOKS

1. Richmond, *The Schaghticoke Nation*, p. 111.
2. Public Records of the State of Connecticut, (1752), p. 108.
3. Wojciechowski, *Ethnohistory*, p. 86.
4. Atwater, *History of Kent*, p. 78.
5. De Forest, *Indians of Connecticut*, p. 418.
6. Public Records of the State of Connecticut, (1801), p. 250.
7. Richmond, *The Schaghticoke Nation*, p. 106.
8. Ibid., p. 106.
9. Smith, J., *History of Dutchess County*, p. 482–483.
10. Wojciechowski, *Ethnohistory*, p. 88.
11. Ibid., p. 88.
12. Ibid., p. 89.
13. Richmond, *The Schaghticoke Nation*, p. 107.
14. Smith, D., *Martyrs*, p. 36.
15. Wojciechowski, *Ethnohistory*, p. 87.
16. De Forest, *Indians of Connecticut*, p. 410.
17. Ibid., p. 410.
18. Smith, D., *Martyrs*, p. 85.
19. De Forest, *Indians of Connecticut*, p. 410–411; Wojciechowski, *Ethnohistory*, p. 91.
20. Richmond, *The Schaghticoke Nation*, p. 110.
21. Public Records of the State of Connecticut, (1778), p. 150.
22. Public Records of the State of Connecticut, (1783), p. 178.
23. Atwater, *History of Kent*, p. 78.

24. De Forest, *Indians of Connecticut*, p. 418.
25. Public Records of the State of Connecticut, (1801), p. 86.
26. Public Records of the State of Connecticut, (1786), p. 255.
27. Public Records of the State of Connecticut, (1801), p. 86, 250.
28. Kent Deeds, Book 10, p. 318–319.
29. Atwater, *History of Kent*, p. 78; De Forest, *Indians of Connecticut*, p. 419.
30. Kent Deeds, Book 10, p. 318–319; Kent Deeds, Book 11, p. 366.
31. Public Records of the State of Connecticut, (1801, Appendix), p. 458.

CHAPTER TEN: THE SCATTERING
THE UNITED STATES IN 1800

1. Adams, *United States in 1800*, p. 11.
2. Ibid., p. 16.
3. Ibid., p. 3.
4. Ibid., p. 12.
5. Ibid., p. 31.
6. Public Records of the State of Connecticut, (1803), p. 249.
7. Public Records of the State of Connecticut, (1810), p. 63.
8. Ibid., p. 63; Kent Deeds, Book 12, p. 520.
9. Kent Deeds, Book 13, p. 113.
10. Kent Deeds, Book 11, p. 82–83.
11. Account Book of Scatacook Indians, 1801–1852, Connecticut State Library.
12. Public Records of the State of Connecticut, (1811), p. 216.
13. Public Records of the State of Connecticut, (1811), p. 198; Slosson, *History*, p. 6.
14. Orcutt, *Indians*, p. 200.
15. Benton, *Oblong Valley*, p. 14.
16. Johnson, P., *Town of Russia*, p. 3.
17. Ibid., p. 2.
18. Ibid., p. 2.
19. Benton, *History of Herkimer County*, p. 491.
20. Van Hoosear, *Fillow-Philleo*, p. 67–69, 73.
21. Russell, *Farming in New England*, p. 147.
22. *New York Times*, October 21, 2003, p. F–2.
23. Survey map of Martin Preston's Lands in author's possession.
24. Estate of David Preston, Dutchess County Surrogate's File # Book 0, p. 503.

25. Office of the Dutchess County Clerk, Deed Liber, 53, p. 285.
26. Kent Deeds, Book 10, p. 419; Kent Deeds, Book 9, p. 374.

CHAPTER ELEVEN: IRON, WOOD, AND LAND
1. Hopson, *Iron Fever*, p. 39.
2. Kirby, *Echoes of Iron*, p. 14.
3. Ibid., p. 14.
4. Hopson, *Iron Fever*, p. 47.
5. Ibid., p. 47.
6. Ibid., p. 47.
7. Leggett, *Patchin Family*, p. 619.
8. Kent Deeds, Book 15, p. 324.
9. Kent Deeds, Book 17, p. 71.
10. Kent Deeds, Book 20, p. 658
11. Kent Deeds, Book 16, p. 359.
12. Kent Deeds, Book 26, p. 26.
13. Office of the Dutchess County Clerk, Deed Liber 36, p. 404.
14. Office of the Dutchess County Clerk, Deed Liber 39, p. 83.
15. Office of the Dutchess County Clerk, Deed Liber 47, p. 397.
16. Office of the Dutchess County Clerk, Deed Liber 49, p. 466.
17. Office of the Dutchess County Clerk, Deed Liber 55, p. 236.
18. Office of the Dutchess County Clerk, Deed Liber 125, p. 65.
19. Office of the Dutchess County Clerk, Deed Liber 38, p. 119.
20. Estate of London Hill, Dutchess County Surrogate Box # 914.
21. Dover Town Records Transcript in author's possession.
22. Office of the Dutchess County Clerk, Deed Liber 38, p. 119.

CHAPTER TWELVE: OUT OF THE SMOKE OF THEIR CHIMNEYS
1. Dutchess County Surrogate File # 1423.
2. Office of the Dutchess County Clerk, Deed Liber 59, p. 56.
3. Dutchess County Surrogate File # 1423.
4. Office of the Dutchess County Clerk, Deed Liber 53, p. 285.
5. Office of the Dutchess County Clerk, Deed Liber 59, p. 59.
6. Dutchess County Surrogate File # 1423.
7. Leggett, *Patchin Family*, p. 608.
8. Ibid., p. 621.
9. Ibid., p. 621.
10. Ibid., p. 653–654.
11. Ibid., p. 656.

12. Ibid., p. 654.
13. Ibid., p. 653.
14. Ibid., p. 618.
15. Dutchess County Surrogate File # Book 0, p. 503.
16. Friedman, *History of American Law*, p. 213.
17. Office of the Dutchess County Clerk, Deed Liber 33, p. 324; Office of the Dutchess County Clerk, Deed Liber 50, p. 10.
18. Office of the Dutchess County Clerk, Deed Liber 35, p. 226; Van Hoosear, *Fillow-Philleo*, p. 105.
19. Pension Application of Isaac Jones, Reel 0720.
20. Pension Application of Silas Curtis, Reel 0720.
21. Pension Application of Darius Cook, Reel 0720.

CHAPTER THIRTEEN: THE CIVIL WAR: TIS NOBLE THUS TO DIE
1. Office of the Dutchess County Clerk, Deed Liber 97, p. 232.
2. 1850 Federal Census, Dover, New York.
3. 1860 Federal Census.
4. Smith, J., *History of Dutchess County*, p. 143.
5. Ibid., p. 144.
6. Atwater, *History of Kent*, p. 38.
7. McPherson, *Battle Cry*, p. 326; Atwater, *History of Kent*, p. 38 et seq.
8. McPherson, *Battle Cry*, p. 330.
9. Ibid., p. 344.
10. Genealogy of John Wolcott and narrative of his escape from Andersonville Prison provided by John B. Wolcott of Corvallis, Oregon, Registrar of the Wolcott Society.
11. Wolverine Brigade website: users.aol.com/dlharvey/michbrigade.htm
12. McPherson, *Battle Cry*, p. 296.
13. Andersonville website: http//www.itd.nps.gov/cwss.
14. The National Park Service website confirms both Wolcott and Barrows escaped.
15. Barrow's account: see Note 10.
16. Ibid.
17. Ibid.
18. Ibid.
19. Ibid.
20. Ibid.
21. Pension Application of Susan Dingee.
22. New York State Agricultural Census of 1865.

23. Pension Application of Susan Dingee.
24. Catton, *Civil War*, p. 15.
25. Ibid., p. 16.
26. Dunbar family information provided by Fran and Ray Smith of New Milford, Connecticut.
27. McPherson, *Battle Cry*, p. 485, 487.
28. Elmira Prison Website: http://www.rootsweb.com/nychemun/prison.htm

CHAPTER FOURTEEN: BLOWED OUT FOR GOOD
1. Pension Application of Susan Dingee.
2. Ibid.
3. Ibid.; Office of the Dutchess County Clerk, Deed Liber 182, p. 203.
4. Office of the Dutchess County Clerk, Deed Liber 133, p. 50.
5. Office of the Dutchess County Clerk, Deed Liber 140, p. 617; Office of the Dutchess County Clerk, Deed Liber 198, p. 82.
6. Friedman, *History of American Law,* p. 208.
7. Ibid., p. 208.
8. Ibid., p. 251.
9. Ibid., p. 211.
10. Office of the Dutchess County Clerk, Deed Liber 244, p. 50.
11. 1875 New York Agricultural Census, Town of Dover.
12. Office of the Dutchess County Clerk, Deed Liber 228, p. 366 (Sabrina Wheeler's will).
13. Russell, *Farming in New England*, p. 256.
14. Ibid., p. 256.
15. Ibid., p. 256.
16. 1865 and 1875 New York Agricultural Censuses, Town of Dover.
17. Location of farms by 1867 Beers Atlas Map.
18. Office of the Dutchess County Clerk, Deed Liber 140, p. 618; Office of the Dutchess County Clerk, Deed Liber 171, p. 389; Office of the Dutchess County Clerk, Deed Liber 171, p. 391.
19. Polhemus, History of Dover, p. 38 (See Note 7, Chapter 11)
20. Kirby, *Echoes of Iron*, p. 61, 117.
21. Hopson, *Iron Fever*, p. 51.

CHAPTER FIFTEEN: THE END OF AN ERA
1. 1880 federal census.
2. Birch, A.W., *Yankee Magazine*, September 1973, p. 112.

3. Office of the Dutchess County Clerk, Deed Liber 301, p. 51.
4. Office of the Dutchess County Clerk, Deed Liber 334, p. 232.
5. 1880 federal census.
6. Johnson, F., *Kent Families*, not paged.
7. Birch, A.W., *Yankee Magazine*, September 1973, p. 194.
8. *Poughkeepsie Sunday Courier*, November 11, 1922, p. 1.
9. Chase, *Sherm Chase Remembers*, p. 13.
10. Birch, A. W., *Yankee Magazine*, September 1973, p. 113.
11. Polhemus, *History of Dover*, p. 38.
12. Leggett, *Patchin Family*, p. 660.
13. Chase, *Sherm Chase Remembers*, p. 11.
14. *Poughkeepsie Sunday Courier*, November 11, 1922, p. 1.
15. Office of the Dutchess County Clerk, Deed Liber 384, p. 253; Office of the Dutchess County Clerk, Deed Liber 384, p. 251; Office of the Dutchess County Clerk, Deed Liber 360, p. 69.
16. Office of the Dutchess County Clerk, Deed Liber 360, p. 242; Office of the Dutchess County Clerk, Deed Liber 447, p. 93; Office of the Dutchess County Clerk, Deed Liber 474, p. 435; Office of the Dutchess County Clerk, Deed Liber 501, p. 304.
17. Office of the Dutchess County Clerk, Deed Liber 464, p. 482.
18. Office of the Dutchess County Clerk, Deed Liber 491, p. 388; Office of the Dutchess County Clerk, Deed Liber 504, p. 323.
19. Chase, *Sherm Chase Remembers*, p. 55.
20. Leggett, *Patchin Family*, p. 660.

Bibliography

Adams, Henry. *The United States in 1800.* Ithaca, NY: Cornell University Press, 1962.

Atwater, Francis. *History of Kent, Connecticut.* Meriden, CT: The Journal Publishing Co., 1897.

Benson, Arthur T. *Jacob Benson, Pioneer: And His Descendants in the Towns of Dover and Amenia, Dutchess County, New York and Elsewhere.* Poughkeepsie, NY: the A.V. Haight Company, 1915.

Benton, Myron B. *Indians of the Oblong Valley.* Originally published in *The Lakeville Journal*; Retrieved from Adriance Library, Local History Room, Poughkeepsie, NY, 1912.

Benton, Nathaniel S. *A History of Herkimer County.* Albany, NY: J. Munsell's Sons, 1856.

Catton, Bruce. *Reflections on the Civil War.* New York: Berkeley Books, 1981.

Chase, Sherman. *Kent Tales: Sherm Chase Remembers: A Kent Life 1900 to 1982.* Kent, CT: The Kent Historical Society, 1991.

De Crevecoeur, J. Hector St. John. *Letters from an American Farmer and Sketches of Eighteenth Century America.* New York: Penguin Classics Ed., 1986.

De Forest, John W. *History of the Indians of Connecticut: From the Earliest Known Period to 1850.* Hartford, CT: Connecticut Historical Society, 1853.

Doherty, Frank J. *Settlers of the Beekman Patent: Dutchess County, New York*, Volumes I, II, III, IV, V, & VI. Pleasant Valley, NY: Frank J. Doherty, Publisher, 1990 et seq.

Feder, Kenneth L. *A Village of Outcasts: Historical Archaeology and Documentary Research at the Lighthouse Site.* Mountain View, CA: Mayfield Publishing Company, 1994.

Flexner, James Thomas. *Washington: The Indispensable Man.* New York: New American Library, 1979.

Friedman, Lawrence M. *A History of American Law*, 2nd ed. New York: Simon & Schuster, 1985.

Griffen, Robert C. and Mitchell R. Alegre. *Wolcott Genealogy.* N.p.: Society of the Descendents of Henry Wolcott, 1986.

Hodges, Graham Russell. *Root and Branch: African Americans in New York and East Jersey, 1613–1863.* Chapel Hill, NC: The University of North Carolina Press, 1999.

Hopson, Emily M., ed. *Kent Tales: Iron Fever: The Iron Industry Permeates Kent.* Kent, CT: The Kent Historical Society, Inc., 1990.

Johnson, Francelia C. *A Register of Some of the Families that Have Lived in Kent, CT, 1739–1999.* Kent, CT: Francelia C. Johnson, Publisher, 2000.

Johnson, Paula. *Town of Russia: Roads.* Russia, NY: The Town of Russia, NY, 2001.

Kammen, Michael. *Colonial New York: A History.* New York: Charles Scribner's Sons, 1975.

Kim, Sung Bok. *Landlord and Tenant in Colonial New York Manorial Society, 1664–1773.* Chapel Hill, NC: The University of North Carolina Press, 1978.

Kirby, Edward M. *Echoes of Iron in Connecticut's Northwest Corner.* Sharon, CT: The Sharon Historical Society, 1998.

Leggett, Grace Patchen. *The History and Genealogy of the Patchin-Patchen Family.* N.p.: The Patchin-Patchen Family Association, 1952.

Lynd, Stoughton. *Anti-Federalism in Dutchess County, New York.* Chicago: Loyola University Press, 1962.

Mark, Irving. *Agrarian Conflicts in Colonial New York: 1711–1775*, 2nd ed. New York: Ira J. Friedman, Inc., 1965.

Martin, Joseph Plumb. *A Narrative of a Revolutionary Soldier.* New York: New American Library, 2001.

McCracken, Henry Noble. *Old Dutchess Forever! The Story of an American County.* New York: Hastings House, 1956.

McPherson, James M. *Battle Cry of Freedom: The Civil War Era.* New York: Ballantine Books, 1988.

Moulton, Phillips P., ed. *The Journal and Major Essays of John Woolman.* Richmond, IN: Friends United Press, 1989.

New-York Historical Society. *Collections of "The Colden Papers" for the Year 1920.* New York: New-York Historical Society, 1921.

Orcutt, Samuel. *The Indians of the Housatonic and Naugatuck Valleys.* Hartford, CT: Case, Lockwood & Brainard Company, 1882.

Parkman, Francis. *Montcalm & Wolfe.* New York: The Modern Library, 1999.

Polhemus, John F. *A History of Dover Township: First Segment.* Dover, NY: Town of Dover Historical Society, 1982.

Poucher, MD, J. Wilson, and Helen Wilkinson Reynolds. "Old Gravestones of Dutchess County, New York," in *Collections of The Dutchess County Historical Society*, vol. 2. Poughkeepsie, NY: The Dutchess County Historical Society, 1924.

Preston, Charles Henry. *Descendants of Roger Preston of Ipswich and Salem Village.* Salem, MA: The Essex Institute, 1931.

Reed, Newton. *Early History of Amenia*, 4th ed. Amenia, NY: Harlem Valley Times, Inc., 1985.

Regents of the State of New York, eds., *Boundaries of the State of New York*. Albany, NY: New York State Regents, 1874.

Reynolds, Helen Wilkinson. "Notices of Marriages and Deaths, About 4,080 in Number, Published in Newspapers Printed in Poughkeepsie, NY: 1778–1825," in *Collections of The Dutchess County Historical Society*, vol. 4. Poughkeepsie, NY: The Dutchess County Historical Society, 1930.

Richmond, Trudie Lamb. "A Narrative Perspective of History: The Schaghti-coke Nation, Resistance and Survival," in *Enduring Traditions: The Native Peoples of New England*, ed. Laurie Weinstein. Westport, CT: Bergin & Garvey, 1994.

Roach, Marilynne E. *The Salem Witch Trials*. New York: Cooper Square Press, 2002.

Russell, Howard S. *A Long Deep Furrow: Three Centuries of Farming in New England*. Hanover, NH: University Press of New England, 1982.

Rust, Albert D. *Record of the Rust Family*. Waco, TX: Albert D. Rust, Publisher, 1891.

Shecter, Barnet. *The Battle for New York: The City at the Heart of the American Revolution*. New York: Penguin Books, 2002.

Scheer, George F., and Hugh F. Rankin, *Rebels and Redcoats*. New York: New American Library, 1957.

Sedgwick, Charles F. *General History of the Town of Sharon, Litchfield County, Connecticut*, 2nd ed. Amenia, NY: Charles Walsh, Printer and Publisher, 1877.

Seymour, Mabel. *A Lawyer of Kent: Barzillai Slosson and His Account Books, 1794–1812*. New Haven, CT: Yale University Press, 1935.

Smith, Chard Powers. *The Housatonic: Puritan River*, The Rivers of Amenia Series. New York: Rinehart & Co., Inc., 1946.

Smith, DeCost. *Martyrs of the Oblong and Little Nine*. Caldwell, ID: The Caxton Printers, Ltd., 1948.

Smith, James H. *A History of Dutchess County, New York*. Rochester, NY: D. Mason & Co., 1882.

Van Hoosear, D. H. *The Fillow, Philo and Philleo Genealogy: A Record of the Descendants of John Fillow, a Huguenot Refugee from France*. Albany, NY: J. Munsell's Sons, 1888.

Wilson, Warren H. *Quaker Hill*, 2nd ed. Pawling, NY: Akin Hall Association, 1987.

Wojciechowski, Franz Laurens. *Ethnohistory of the Paugussett Tribes: Exercise in*

Research Methodology. Amsterdam, Netherlands: Kira Monograph Series, 1992.

Wood, Gordon S. *The American Revolution: A History.* New York: Modern Library, 2002.

Wood, Gordon S. *The Radicalism of the American Revolution.* New York: Vintage Books Division of Random House, 1993.

Index

Haggerty, Ed 161
Hancock County (IL) 130-131
Harrington, _____ 63
Harrington, Abel 75
Harrington, George 22
Harrington, Mary 22
Hawley & Co. 31, 34-35
Hector, George 145-146
Hill, _____ 90, 113, 121, 153
Hill, Bethany 84
Hill, Caleb 84
Hill, Caleb (son of London) 84, 86-87, 122
Hill, Grace 121-122
Hill, Henry 91
Hill, Joseph 91, 122
Hill, London 82, 84, 88, 90-91, 121
Hill, London, Jr. 86
Hill, Richard 122
Hill, Ruth 88
Hilton, Claire 163
Hoffman, Col. William 147
Holdridge, Daniel 145
Holt, Nicholas 24
Honey 18, 64
Hoofcoot see Hufcut
Hopson, Stuart 120
Hopson, William Trapp 115, 118, 157
Housatonic River 20, 46-48, 68, 97-98, 100, 115
Hoveout, The 16, 32-36, 39
Howland, Azariah 133
Hoyt, Nathan 28
Hubbell, Jedediah 39
Hubble see Hubbell
Hudson River 20, 29-30, 42
Hufcut, _____ 92

Hufcut, Erroll 158
Hufcut, George 121-122, 153
Hufcut, Henry 157
Hufcut, Henry J. 135, 153-158, 169
Hufcut, Patty 135
Hufcut, Preston 153-157
Humeston, Joe 161
Hurricane of 1815 111

Ipswich (MA) 24
Iron Industry 115-123

Jackson, _____ 90, 113, 153
Jackson, Michael 74, 89, 91, 120, 123
Jewitt, John 124
Johnson, John 133
Johnson, Paula 108
Jones, Anna 133-134
Jones, Issac 133-134
Judd, Philip 16

Kelley, Wing 43
Kempe, William 34-35
Kenedy see Kennedy
Kennedy, _____ 55, 155
Kennedy, Alan 129
Kennedy, Allen P. 82, 112-113, 118, 124, 128, 132, 135, 153-158, 160, 169
Kennedy, Archibald 31, 33
Kennedy, David 113, 132
Kennedy, Elizabeth 57, 82, 124
Kennedy, Eliza 132
Kennedy, Erben 7-8, 132, 161-165
Kennedy, Francis 128, 132
Kennedy, Gideon 57-58, 82
Kennedy, Hugh 57-58

Acknowledgments

M ANY PEOPLE HELPED US to research and write this book. The folks at the Kent Historical Society were generous with their time and counsel. We particularly thank Suze Williams and Marge McAvoy. The late Emily Hopson often consulted her memory on our behalf, and her memory contained a treasury of local history. We sought material at the Quaker Hill Historical Society, the Litchfield County Historical Society, and the New-York Historical Society in Manhattan. Paula Johnson, historian of the town of Russia, New York, was especially helpful in finding information about our subjects who had emigrated there. Some of the material in the book was developed from resources of the Dover Historical Society for the book *The History of Dover Township*.

Descendants and relatives of Mountain people often proved to be our best resource. We are indebted to Keith Smith of Aurora, Colorado, for information about the Philleos; to John Wolcott of Corvallis, Oregon, Emily Haas of Norwalk, Connecticut, and Ken Adam of Groton, Connecticut, for Wolcott family material; to John Patchin of the Patchin(en) Family Association; and to Lou Twitty of Chino Valley, Arizona for Patchin family history. We owe a special thanks for the efforts and warm hospitality of Ray and Fran Smith of New Milford, Connecticut, in helping us research the Dunbar family.

Several people aided our physical research on the Mountain; they often became companions in our search. We are particularly grateful for the friendship and guidance of the late Darwin Benson and the late Elmer Wyman. Horatio Benson and Richard Wyman also helped greatly in our explorations of the forest. And we are grateful to Robert J. Keller, Jim and Jeanne Muncey, and Larry Whitford for their help and kindness.

All historians and history-lovers in Dutchess County now have a priceless resource in Frand Doherty's monumental, multi-volume work, *Settlers of the Beekman Patent*. In addition to the exhaustive genealogical material, Doherty's volumes contain collections of transcriptions of original documents, including such things as the minutes of the Oblong Friends Meeting, military rolls, and metes and bounds descriptions of the early roads. We have quoted Mr. Doherty liberally and we thank him for his work.

We thank Julie and Jenn Polhemus: Julie for her photographs, her hand-drawn maps, and lots of good advice; Jenn for her work in preparing the manuscript and for much-need technical advice.

Tamara Zipperle cheerfully met the challenge of preparing the manuscript from our drafts.

We express our appreciation to Wray and Loni Rominger of Purple Mountain Press and their copyeditor Aileen Weintraub.

Finally, we want to thank our wives, Gayle and Maria, for their patience through this long process.

PURPLE MOUNTAIN PRESS, a publishing company established in 1973, is committed to producing the best books of regional interest as well as bringing back into print significant older works. For a free catalog, write Purple Mountain Press, Ltd., P.O. Box 309, Fleischmanns, NY 12430; or call (845) 254-4062; or fax (845) 254-4476; or email purple@catskill.net. On the web at www.catskill.net/purple.